POLICE BLOTTER
Kaua'i style

by GEORGIA MOSSMAN

POLICE BLOTTER
Kaua'i Style

© Copyright 2000 by Georgia Mossman. All rights reserved.

No part of this publication may be reproduced, stored in a retrieval system, or transmitted, in any form or by any means – electronic, mechanical, photocopying, recording, or otherwise, without the prior written permission of the publisher.

Printed in the United States of America.
Second printing 2008

Published by

Ka Hui Kanelimu
5968 Heamoi Place
Kapa'a, Kaua'i, Hawai'i 96746

Library of Congress Catalog Card No: 00-191701

ISBN: 0-9702873-0-5

This book is dedicated to:

Ralph J. Mossman
Whose encouragement, sense of humor, and great cartoons took this from a much talked-about project, to a completed manuscript

to:
Reyn, Nicholas and Allegra Mossman
(the amazing Next Generation)

and to
The wonderful people of Kauaʻi

A Slice of Life in Paradise

Introduction

As a reporter for The Garden Island newspaper I spent more than 20 years chronicling the events listed on the Daily Bulletin of the Kaua'i Police Department. These are excerpts and highlights from the weekly "Police News" and, later, the "Police Blotter" columns that ran in the paper for many years. They are combined with interesting court cases, amusing news stories, "Off the Record" items, and thoughts and observations from the years I spent at the police station and in the courts.

One doesn't need to know the cast of characters to be able to relate to these tales. They are small-town stories enriched by a multicultural populace. They are a microcosm of human foibles and more serious character flaws, of kindness, meanness, stories filled with pathos, and many that are downright funny.

They represent only one slice of life in paradise. Naturally, because they come from police records, they don't tell the story of the majority of good people who live on this beautiful island out in the middle of the Pacific Ocean.

While these tales were gathered over two decades, many are from the late 1970s and early 1980s, a time when there was a great deal more tolerance of drinking and drugs, when there was about an equal number of churches and bars, when life on Kauaʻi was a lot more laid back. It was also a time when the KPD didn't keep tallies on the number of citations issued and arrests its officers made.

And despite this "evidence to the contrary," Kauaʻi is really a safe place to live and visit. There are certainly more thefts than there should be, but when it comes to violent crime, Hawaiʻi is one of the safest places in the country and the island of Kauaʻi has the lowest crime rate in the state, by far.

Georgia Mossman

Kapaʻa, Kauaʻi, Hawaiʻi

Acknowledgments

My deepest appreciation goes to the officers and staff of the Kaua'i Police Department who for 20 years answered my questions, went in search of files, provided leads, and in general tolerated my constant presence with, for the most part, grace, good humor and friendship.

It's hard to narrow down the list, but lest their extra efforts seem unappreciated, I want to acknowledge Chief (ret.) Brian Fujiuchi, Chief George Freitas, Inspector (ret.) Wayne Tanaka, Inspector (ret.) Dennis Higashi, Inspector Mel Morris, (all ret.); Former Lts. Marty Curnan and Bill Ching, and Pat Layosa.

Special thanks also to Records Supervisor Estelle Furuike and members of her staff over the years who have gone "above and beyond" to help me; and to the patrolmen and sergeants, those on the front line who were always willing to share their stories, some sad and some zany, and bring me up to speed on what was happening around the island.

It's hard to imagine that reporters elsewhere had as much assistance and cooperation as I received over the years, from Jodie Nishino, Judges Kei Hirano (ret.) and George "Spike" Masuoka (ret.); Millie Ah Hee (ret.) and all the staff members at the Fifth Circuit Courts; and Bailiff Georgia Lomasad;

(former) Deputy Prosecutor Al Castillo, his fellow prosecutors and their support staff; (former) Prosecutor Mike Soong; and Public Defender, the esteemed Jim Jung, and his attorneys and staff.

I think of you as friends as well as associates. Mahalo nui loa to you all.

William LeGro organized this material from the thousands of stories I've written over the years, and really got the book started and the author moving. His help and encouragement is truly appreciated.

When I look at what I've written and recall the interesting experiences behind the columns and the stories, I realize they've helped shape who I've become. Because I'm not unhappy with the results, I thank Jean Holmes, my editor at *The Garden Island*, who taught me the news business. Jean was like those sharp, hard-working news hounds you saw in some of the old-time movies. She has remained a wonderful friend who has provided support and wise counsel on both professional and personal matters for lo these many years.

Very Important People also are Ralph, Brad and Jay Mossman, who tolerated my long hours and a job that consumed so much of my time and interest. And I apologize for all the times a glazed look came over my eyes as you were talking to me while I had one ear glued to the police radio scanner. One couldn't ask for a nicer family.

Also major influences on my life and times over the past 30 years have been Violet and Bill Chu (deceased), many members of the large and wonderful Kaʻauwai ʻohana and Louise Marston (deceased) of Tahiti Nui in Hanalei. They personify aloha and have greatly enriched my life.

Finally, a special thanks to all the cops and criminals, saints and sinners, drunks and druggies, fighting families and naked nuts, tourists and titas who have made my Kaua'i community such a warm and wonderful, funny place to live – and my job the best on the planet. I love you all.

The Island of Kaua'i

TABLE OF CONTENTS

ABOUT KAUAʻI	21
BASICS FROM THE BLOTTER	25
AS I SEE IT	41
AIN'T LOVE GRAND	43
OFF THE RECORD	52
HOLOHOLONA (assorted animals)	57
WHAT'S MINE IS YOURS	75
OFF THE RECORD, AGAIN	80
THE COPS WHO COULDN'T SHOOT STRAIGHT	83
WE TOO HAVE LOST SOULS	87
A BANK ROBBERY, JUST FOR PRACTICE	90
HIGH-TIMES AND MISDEMEANORS	96
PAKALOLO EVERYWHERE YOU TURN	102
OVERHEARD ON THE SCANNER	105
COPS 'N' ROBBERS	108
MISCELLANEOUS KINE REPORTS	112
THE NAKED BLOTTER	117
GAMBLING IS A WAY OF LIFE	121
SENTENCES TO MAKE YOU THINK	127
KAUAI'S KEIKI	133
VISITORS AND WAYFARERS	142
GLOSSARY	152

About Kaua'i

The Garden Island's 555 square miles, together with the private "Forbidden Island" of Ni'ihau (72 square miles), are Kaua'i County, one of the four counties in the state of Hawai'i and two of the seven main islands. Hawai'i is about 2500 miles from Los Angeles, California and 3800 miles from Tokyo, Japan.

For most of the island's history, sugar was king. Life revolved around the plantations, owned and operated by members of missionary families and enterprising white "foreigners," most of whom came from the United States mainland. Some Germans were hired as the plantation engineers and managers, while *lunas*, or supervisors, were often men who came from Portugal.

The Hawaiians' population had been drastically reduced by disease brought to the islands by sailors and traders. The survivors fished and grew taro and they weren't about to change their way of life just because the white man needed people to work in their cane fields.

So, with thousands and thousands of acres of prime land to be planted and harvested and virtually no laborers available locally, emissaries went first to China, then Japan and Korea, and later the Philippines, to hire men to work in the fields.

The labor contracts included provisions for housing so the plantations built small homes in camps, and workers were assigned as they arrived, often as a group of the same nationality, to a specific camp. Soon the camps began to be identified according to the majority of workers from the Orient who lived there. That led to their being referred to as the *Japanee* or *Pake* (Chinese) camps. There were/are also stereotyped characteristics that accompany that identification (some of which may be accurate), but they are not barriers to friendship. That meant the people of Kaua'i were divided not only by economic class, but also by ethnicity. The Caucasians, referred to as *haoles* (white strangers) were generally well-to-do, and although they were a small minority, the descendants of the missionaries and the plantation managers were the "ruling elite" until World War II.

The result has been that everyone is aware of everyone else's ethnic background and includes it as a part of a description of the person (without a derogatory meaning), which is difficult for newcomers to understand.

In the past 25-30 years, in addition to surviving and rebuilding after two major hurricanes, 'Iwa in 1982 and Iniki in 1992, Kaua'i's population has grown from 30,000 to more than 63,000. Despite this growth, the Garden Island is still basically rural and unsophisticated. Its incredible beauty is marred only by unsuspected dangers in its deceptively serene terrain.

There are now more people and many more cars, but there is still only one main highway (Kuhio/Kaumuali'i) that runs three-quarters of the way around the island. The remaining quarter, the northern coastline, is sheer mountain cliffs, accessible only in good weather and only by boat, plane or hiking trails.

Everyone lives on the fringes of the island, within about 10 miles of the ocean, because the center of the island is a series of beautiful, impenetrable mountains.

The sugar cane industry is slowly dying and there is an attempt being made to plant former cane lands in a variety of crops, but tourism is the island's number one industry. And with about 15,000 visitors on the island each day, they too play a role in this particular slice of life.

For words or phrases that are unfamiliar or are unique to Kaua'i or Hawai'i, there is a glossary at the back of the book.

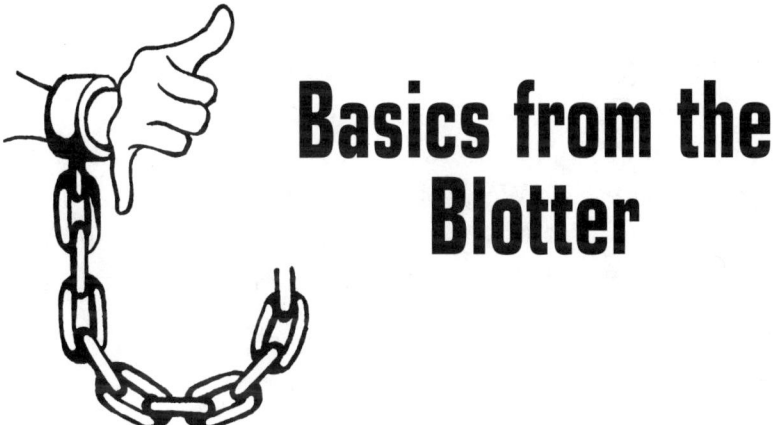

Basics from the Blotter

Every call the police dispatcher receives is given a number and noted in a sentence or two, on the Daily Bulletin, *and the number of calls now exceeds more than 20,000 each year. I culled what I thought was interesting from that Bulletin listing, then went seeking answers to questions and clarification when possible. I also tried to follow-up on tips I picked up from my crackling radio scanner at home.*

My sources were usually cooperative but sometimes the report wasn't completed, the officer who handled the call just finished his shift or went on his three days off, etc., etc., so I and the readers were left with tantalizing tidbits and mysteries.

These are samples of what appeared in my newspaper columns, complete with accompanying editorial comments.

Hangings reported... police received a report of what appeared to be a body hanging from a tree at the Old Marine (Corps) Camp in Wailua. It turned out to be an inflatable sex doll. Officers removed the doll (and disposed of it, we presume?)... and if you've heard the rumor that there were two bodies hanging from a tree at Mango Tree Pond near the Loop Road in Wailua, please call the police because they haven't heard anything about it and don't like to be left in the dark.

Requests for removal... Someone called police to remove an "unwanted" drunk (is there ever a "wanted" drunk?) from a bar in Poʻipu, from a church, a Waipouli restaurant, Aunty Margaret's bar on the West side, a Lihuʻe motel, a North Shore resort, and a Kapaʻa bar (it's not that we have so many unwanteds but the unwanteds tend to move from place to place, because they're unwanted).

Sweet-talkers... A complaint that some local guys were harassing a New York photographer's models on the beach at Hanamaʻulu Bay (and we can hear those smooth talkers now)... a caller said a strange man dressed like Jesus was roaming around the Lihuʻe area... and a security guard at the Fun Factory in Kapaʻa was playing with his handcuffs and put them on a customer, then couldn't find the key, so the manager had to call police to free the little guy.

Loud grazers... A jailer at the "Wailua Hilton" (the correctional center) reported hearing strange noises at the golf course across Kuhio Hwy., and officers found a wild boar grazing on the #10 tee ... a concerned caller said a neighbor lady who is getting "old-timer's disease" was using a machete to cut down all her (own) pretty flowers... there was a call saying two men atop a roof in Nawiliwili were fighting with 2 x 4s... and someone made off with two bags of fertilizer that belonged to Rex, who calls himself the "King of Dung."

Beware of survey-takers... Police got a report of a man wearing a turban claiming he was doing a survey for the Department of Social Services, then once he was seated in the subject's parlor, he exposed himself. Word from DSS is that they aren't taking any surveys and to beware of men in turbans exposing themselves… and there was a request for police to deliver a message to a member of a visiting parachute jumping team, and it was duly noted that the message had been left taped to the airplane.

False impressions… There was a hurry-up call for police to investigate a report of three men at the Market Place in Wailua, dressed in camouflage and carrying what appeared to be live ammunition, but it turned out to be three actors working on the movie being filmed here, "Uncommon Valor," who were taking a shopping break.

Argument amongst the tombstones… A late-night caller said there was a big argument going on at the Japanese Cemetery, but it turned out to be beings-still-of-this-earth involved in a heated discussion… police received a report of a strange male sitting on the sidewalk near Lihu'e Shopping Center, (proving everything is relative, because people are used to seeing a strange *female* sitting there).

Anxious to be free… we checked on two men we saw hitchhiking in Wailua shortly after midnight, and learned that the pair had finished serving their time at the jail at 12:01 a.m. and they wanted to be released immediately. They obviously did not want to take advantage of the state's hospitality one more minute than necessary, transportation or no transportation.

A local refrain… When officers responded to a report of an assault in progress outside the Hanalei Police Substation, the people gathered outside told them, "Sure we was a witness, we nevah see nothin"… and the same response came from people at a house in Puhi when police answered a call about a fight and gunshots.

Another "blind" witness… A man said he was attacked for no reason known to him as he came out of a Nawiliwili restaurant; his assailant punched him in the eye, which swelled shut almost immediately, and since he's blind in the other eye, he couldn't give police much of a description… and a Kekaha man called to say he was assaulted by "unknown," but it turned out that he had called in advance, fearing he was going to be the "assaultee," but the disagreement had been settled by the time police arrived.

Screaming was her M.O.… Police responded to a report of a woman screaming in Lawa'i, but when they got there she screamed that she didn't need their assistance… we trust that the report that a "driver ran over a light pole" meant that the pole was lying on the ground… and a vehicle from Rent-a-Wreck was involved in an accident (so does that make it More-of-a-Wreck?).

Was it a dream?… A Kapa'a woman said she thought she had been raped two nights before. She said she had taken a sleeping pill, and the next morning she had the feeling that someone had broken into her home and taken advantage of her during the night, but police couldn't find any sign of forced entry.

A browsing burglar… Someone broke into Otsuka's furniture store in Kapa'a, and while some things had been moved around, nothing was missing, so apparently the burglar was just browsing… a Hanalei beat cop lost his "posse box" with his citation books, so if anyone finds it, please… and police picked up a Kapaʻa man who had been AWOL from the military for 14 *years*!

Annie's lost her head… There was a report that someone had screwed the head off Resusci-Annie, and the Red Cross would like that vital part of its CPR dummy returned… and a caretaker in Nawiliwili, cleaning up after his tenant had been whisked off to jail, found a bag with a gun and several thousand dollars in it (which the tenant apparently didn't think wise to take with him), and the honest caretaker turned it over to police.

"Must be a Portagee…" A hunter took his 30.06 rifle out of the case at Lihuʻe Airport to show security people it wasn't loaded, and the shotgun unloaded itself – with the shot hitting (only) a ticket-counter computer… a Hanapepe woman said a man hit her with his guitar (which meant he must have really been mad)… and there was a request for police to check on two men at the Market Place in Wailua, who were, according to the caller, acting like women and went into the shopping center restroom. The officer checked the men's room and didn't find anyone (but maybe he should have checked the *lua* for the *wahine*).

Come on now… A caller from Hanalei who lives along Kuhio Hwy. complained that people stop and use his outdoor shower… even worse, an Anahola woman told police there was a woman in her house, taking a shower, and she doesn't even know her… an elderly lady got into LaFrance Kapaka-Arboleda's car at Hanamaʻulu Store and wouldn't get out, so good-hearted LaFrance had no option but to call police for help… Tetsuo Konishi of Lawa'i said someone removed his good tire and replaced it with an old, flat one… and the owner of a dress shop said she has a problem because someone is looking through the racks and slipping religious literature in the pockets of all her clothing.

Foreplay was the problem… A Kaua'i man reported a woman missing, a lady he'd met and was courting after responding to her ad seeking male companionship, in a Personals column. He told the officer he thought they were getting along nicely, nothing unusual had happened, and he not only didn't know why she left, she hadn't even taken her suitcase with her.

The officer saw nothing to indicate foul play and he didn't know what else to do, so he took the woman's luggage to the station. When they finally contacted the woman, she said being tied-up in a dentist's chair was not her idea of foreplay. She panicked and fled and no way was she coming back to the island. So the police (possibly feeling she was lucky he wasn't really a dentist and not into pain), had no choice but to send her her suitcase.

List that jerk… There were two reports of "illegal touching" intended to be "for record only," from the YWCA's Sexual Assault Center. This means the victim doesn't want to pursue the report now but she does want the police to have the name and address of this jerk, in case he continues being a jerk.

Hawaiians with spears… A frantic caller from Wainiha said about 50 people with guns and knives had come to take over his property. Blue-and-whites started flying, stopping only at Hanalei substation for rifles. But there was no one at the property when they arrived. Investigation revealed that a group of Niʻihau Hawaiians from the West side had gotten permission from the landowner to go through his property to trek into the mountains for ʻopae (shrimp) and wi (tamarinds). They were no doubt carrying spears and knives and, though possibly startling, were no threat to anyone.

Strangers in a strange place... A report that caused some concern, was a rare occurrence on the island of Niʻihau, which is about 20 miles off Kauaʻi.

Only Hawaiians who live there are allowed to come ashore so when a haole couple walked into the village, the local folks made a call on the radio to the Robinsons on Kauaʻi, the family that owns the island. Bruce Robinson then called police to report trespassers on Niʻihau.

Robinson, combining caution with paranoia, had the villager take the woman, in the dinghy, back to the couple's boat. On board, the villager verified her identity, that they truly were from the mainland and that they were in need of drinking water. So the couple was given water and escorted back to their boat, and they no doubt listed their stop on Niʻihau, which they'd learned was also called the forbidden island, in their ship's log, as a strange experience.

What could it be?... There was a report of someone acting strange in Kapaʻa (we couldn't imagine what could be "strange" in Kapaʻa town)... James Silva of Kekaha found a green coffin with brass trimmings at the Kekaha dump... and there was a report of an ultralight that had run out of "gas" with the plane and its pilot "landing" in some trees at Mount Kahili.

Bravery above and beyond... A report of five females fighting at a Kapaʻa bar was no doubt a sight to behold (and it took a brave officer to wade in, break it up, then to try to find out who started it)... and a 3 a.m. caller from Ma's Place in Lihuʻe said someone was pounding on the back door of Hamura's Saimin, and police found a young man who said his pregnant wife was craving saimin, and sorry, but he didn't realize the restaurant was closed.

ʻTis sad... Checking on a late-night report of someone digging in the St. Catherine's Cemetery in Kapaʻa, the officer discovered an elderly man digging a grave for his grandson, who had died that day.

Unless it was you... There was a rash of traffic accidents over the weekend, but all of them were relatively minor except to those involved. And one of them was a policeman who, rushing to The Scene, lost control of his blue-and-white and took part of a newly constructed pasture fence with him.

Plan to get tax-dollar's worth... There was a request for an officer to stand by at the mayor's office because a taxpayer was going to come in to give the mayor a piece of his mind, but he didn't show up (maybe because he didn't have a piece to spare?) ... a caller said a man was chasing cars near Kauaʻi Museum late at night, and it turned out to be a drunk on a bicycle, and because driving under the influence doesn't cover bicycles, police took him home "without incident"... and a Lihuʻe woman said her ex-boyfriend was outside systematically destroying her car with a hammer.

Calls aplenty... Officers were sent to check on barking dogs and noisy pigs; a drunk who lurched through a window at Sueoka's Store in Koloa; and reports of obscene and nuisance phone calls (which is not to say that obscene calls can't be a nuisance).

Ohmigawd!... An Aliomanu woman woke up at 2:30 a.m. and discovered a man she didn't know in bed with her.

She told police that at first she thought the cat had jumped up on the bed. She felt the covers and realized it was a person, and wondered if one of her house mates had gotten into bed with her. She took a look, realized it was a stranger and started screaming. The man said, "I thought you wanted me to come over," then took off. Her screaming awakened the other people in the house and they saw the man running off through the yard.

Troubled souls... A man asked police for assistance with his wife who had barricaded herself in a room with a knife. They were able to convince her she wasn't being poisoned and no one was after her, then they gently put her in the patrol car and took her to Mahelona Hospital for treatment... and a man at a Lihu'e motel asked to speak to an officer because someone was playing with his mind.

Tough love... A concerned mother said her young son was at a neighbor's house smoking pot and would the police do something about it (and they did)... A Kapa'a woman said her husband was having a confrontation with a neighbor and maybe a patrolman could just drive by slowly... and 15 gallons of white paint was spilled on Kuhio Highway near Hanama'ulu, with police getting calls from some of the unsuspecting drivers who drove through it when it was still wet.

Who shot whom?... A doctor in the emergency room at Wilcox Hospital treated a man for a gunshot wound in the shoulder, then got real busy and didn't get around to calling police for several hours. It turned out that by that time the victim had left the hospital and had also left a phony name and address. Police were unable to do a follow-up report because they don't know who was shot, by whom, or why.

Aloha counts... Ron Gilbert of the Trading Post in Lawa'i found the wallet a Japanese visitor forgot at his shop, so he raced to the airport and gave the wallet with the $670 in it to the old man, who had tears in his eyes because he was so touched by Gilbert's gesture of aloha.

She's where?... A (gallant) police officer reported finding a young woman "who somehow fell asleep on the pavement under a truck in the parking lot," and he made arrangements for her to be driven home... a woman wanted to speak to an officer about her pet goat... and a caller from PMRF at Barking Sands reported one of their Navy pilots sighted a 9-foot shark that he thought might be a tiger shark, about 50 yards off the beach at Polihale.

A scary misunderstanding... A mother working in Lihu'e got a frantic call saying her babysitter in Wailua was holding her children at knife point. Police heeded her plea to hurry but they found no serious problem. The sitter was cleaning fish and had a knife in his hand while he was scolding the children.

At 6 years old, no less... A youngster went to a lady's home (twice) and told her he had been beaten by his parents and could he come and live with her. The lady was touched by the story and called police. The officer took the six-year-old to the hospital's emergency room for a thorough examination, but the doctor couldn't find any sign of abuse. When the officer found the little boy's mother, she said her son is talking to someone at the Mental Health Center about his penchant for telling such big, sad stories at such a tender age.

What a surprise! When police responded to a report of a domestic in Kilauea, they were looking in the yard at night for the male member of the battling pair and they were startled when they discovered a three-and-a-half foot iguana.

They confiscated the illegal animal and turned it over to the Agriculture Department in Lihuʻe, and Ed Pickop crated it and sent it on to Honolulu. It's being held as evidence while agriculture officials work with the local prosecutor on the prohibited animals charge against the 29-year-old male. He could face a maximum penalty of $25,000 and a year in jail.

The man said he moved to Kauaʻi only a few weeks ago and had sent the pet iguana through the U.S. Mail, mixed in a box of stuffed animals. He also had a return plane ticket, and officers urged him to use it as soon as possible.

Keep your eyes on the cars... A Traffic Unit officer in a line of cars in the Tunnel of Trees, headed toward Koloa, was keeping his eye on a vehicle that appeared to be swerving, three cars ahead of him. When it looked like the car crossed the centerline, the officer switched on his blue light and started to pull out, to pull the errant driver over. The only problem was that as soon as he switched on his blue light, the drivers in the two cars ahead of him immediately came to a complete stop. So did the officer, after he rear-ended the car in front of him.

A call for thought... Dispatch received a call from an alarm company in Honolulu, asking that an officer check on a home in Poʻipu. The caller said when a burglary alarm went off at that house, they called, and the person who answered the telephone said s/he was a realtor, so don't worry. But the house was empty when the officer arrived. Hmmm... and there were numerous reports of late-night trespassers using the county's latest "vehicle graveyard" in Wailua as an auto parts store.

Where's the proof... An officer checked an open lewdness report from a nurse at Wilcox Hospital, who said a visitor was exposing himself, but the alleged offender claimed he was just tucking in his shirt.... and mental midgets senselessly damaged about 15 rental cars in a Poʻipu resort parking lot; while other members from the same gene pool set a fire in the *lua* at Nawiliwili Park; and some idiot dumped an old refrigerator on Koloa Road.

Dotson delivers - in a Toyota... A 9 lb, 11 oz baby was delivered by Larry Dotson, M.D. this week, in a Toyota pick-up truck parked in front of the Kalaheo fire station. A woman in labor and her husband were making a quick trip from ʻEleʻele to Wilcox Hospital... and they didn't make it.

When it became obvious that there was no time to spare and the couple stopped at the fire station, one of the firemen called Dr. Dotson, who lives in Kalaheo. He happened to be home and he also happened to be the woman's obstetrician. The delivery wasn't as sterile or as private as it might have been, but the audience was enthusiastic and everything went well. Mother, father and baby are doing fine. The folks at the Brick Oven Pizza place across the street were so pleased, they delivered a free celebration pizza to the delivery crew.

Dotson delivers in a Toyota, let's party!

This community backs up its cops... A concerned citizen called to report a police officer having trouble trying to make an arrest at Vidinha Stadium parking lot. It was Officer William Ching, demonstrating how to approach, stop and cuff a suspect to a group of recruits (but it's comforting to know there are citizens out there concerned about helping an officer in distress).

An armed observer... A more "proactive" citizen came upon a similar training session at the stadium. Instead of calling the police, he remained in his truck and pointed a pistol at the man taking the officer "down." That created quite a stir because it looked like a real gun, although it was actually a starter pistol. Recruits got to see a real-life police action as cops disarmed the man and dragged him from his truck. His good intentions kept him from being arrested, but they also could have gotten him shot.

Where there's a hole, there's a guy to fall in it: A caller said two men "fell into the earth and need assistance," but police couldn't find them.

However, another late-night caller said a man had fallen into a big hole in Nawiliwili near the Pier 3 construction site. This time cops and rescue teams did find the man who had fallen into the earth – specifically, an uncovered, unmarked and unlit hole 12-feet deep and 6-feet wide. Doctors at Wilcox Hospital treated the man for back strain and released the lucky guy.

And a Kapaʻa man was walking alongside a hole dug to install a huge utility pole in Kapahi, and of course he fell in – 25 feet to the bottom. Rescue workers pulled him out and took him to Wilcox, where he, too, was treated and released.

No help for library morale... Some punks dropped some firecrackers in the Book Drop at Kapa'a Library, probably thinking it was a harmless prank. It wasn't. Fortunately, the extinguisher in the drop worked and contained the fire, so only the drop and the books it held were ruined. But the fine powder from the extinguisher sprayed the whole library, which had to be closed a full day for cleaning. The entire affair cost taxpayers several thousand dollars.

How rumors get started... Police were startled to get a report of military personnel marching down Hanama'ulu Road harassing neighborhood kids. They investigated and learned that soldiers from O'ahu, here for training and carrying rubber rifles, had marched from Blue Hole at the base of Wai'ale'ale to Lihu'e Airport. Towards the end of this rugged march, on their way through Hanama'ulu, they good-humoredly yelled at some kids as they marched by, asking if they could borrow the kids' skateboards to make their march a little easier. (Hanama'ulu, by the way, means "tired-from-walking bay".)

Canadians can be weird, too: A man who tried to get into jail finally made it – the hard way. Police charged the 28-year-old resident of Vancouver, B.C., with attempted murder and criminal property damage for allegedly crashing his car into a pole that held up a surveillance camera at the Kaua'i Community Correctional Center, and attempting to run down a guard.

When patrolman Foto Agosto, Jr. arrived at the jail, the Canadian was still trying to run down the guard, and each time he missed, he put the car into reverse and tried again. It turns out that the man had first tried to gain entrance to KCCC by telling the guard that he was a CIA agent and would like the names of all of the inmates.

"So... They're like heroes, yeah?"

Wouldn't a fire extinguisher have worked just as well?... There was a car on fire in the parking lot at Princeville Shopping Center, and the unofficial report is that people nearby, anxious to get the burning car out of the lot before it exploded, got carried away and had pushed it across Kuhio Highway and halfway over the cliff at the Hanalei lookout. Unfortunately, the driver was still behind the wheel. Fortunately, the car didn't explode and the driver wasn't badly injured, despite everyone's best efforts.

Can I keep it? A Koloa woman asked to speak to an officer about a human skull she found near Waikomo Stream. (Such finds are not uncommon because ancient Hawaiians were often buried near the ocean, but for the uninitiated, it can certainly be startling!)

As I See It

At the risk of sounding like a National Highway Safety public service message…having seen and written about so many traffic accidents over the years, I am still amazed at how many people are walking away from, or suffering relatively minor injuries in serious wrecks, especially head-on collisions, because of air bags and seat belts.

I've also noticed that the amount of damage to the car or truck in which someone died varies greatly. While the difference in the size and weight of the two vehicles that collide can save or take someone's life, when you see cars with almost no damage, yet people died in that accident, it makes you think about the adage, "When it's your time, it's your time."

About a half-dozen times cars have gone off the road on the sharp curve near Lumahaʻi lookout and plunged 250 feet down the cliff and are found resting, bottom up, with the drivers having survived with maybe just minor injuries, even if it's a little compact car. That makes you think of the adage, "When it's not your time, it's not your time."

In more up-to-date style, a woman doing a daredevil act, driving those treacherous curves to Haʻena and talking on her cellular phone, hit the lava rock wall, then went up over the retainer. Lucky for her she only fell part way down the cliff and (even if it may have been the cause of the accident) she did have a phone handy to call for help.

"Ain't Love Grand"
Family fights, aka Domestics

In 1971, my husband came home and announced we'd just bought Pau Hana, one of the five swinging bars in Kapa'a town. And being haole *(Caucasian) owners of a local bar, at that time and place, turned out to be an amazing experience.*

In those days, few local people entertained in their homes, so the bar was like a social club. Pau Hana sponsored a mountain ball team. My husband made the pupus *(snacks, fish, etc.) that were necessary to the drinking process and we got to know the regulars.*

The local people are generally kind, generous and non-materialistic. There are so many talented people and so many beautiful voices that sometimes there would be fun and music from the time the bar opened until it closed. It was usually a great time, except for the "domestics" or family fights, often provoked or enhanced by a few drinks. Although it was no different and no worse than the other bars in town, Pau Hana was laughingly referred to as the "smallest gymnasium in Kapa'a."

The attitude of the police toward domestics, not just at the bars but all around the island, reflected the attitude of the community and the times. Family fights just weren't criminal matters.

In the years since, Kaua'i has joined the rest of the country in changing its attitude toward drinking and domestics. There's now only one bar in Kapa'a town, and police officers recognize that physical abuse within the family, especially in the family, is a crime. So remember, many of these items are from earlier days.

Learning from experience... The fire department responded to a report of a man taking his ex-wife's clothes out to the front yard and setting them on fire, and police responded also, in anticipation of the "domestic" bound to follow... and a woman called to complain that her neighbors were interfering in the argument she was having with her husband (and it's pretty bad when you can't fight in peace).

Seeking a listening ear... a Kekaha man asked police to swing by and tell his wife to leave him alone while he repairs his boat... and a domestic argument in front of police headquarters ended with the woman angrily backing her car out of the parking space – and smack into a police car.

Planning ahead... Someone requested an officer to be sent to a certain address because of a family fight – but not for half an hour (hmmmm)... police arrested a Lawa'i man on a felony assault charge for running down his wife with their car (and while the injuries were minor, that kind of thing can be dangerous)... and there was a call for police assistance when a mainland man began beating up his wife at the Seaflite Terminal in Nawiliwili – so the officer gave her a ride to the airport when she wisely decided to leave by air and let her husband take a slow boat (a hydrofoil) to Honolulu.

Who knows why some guys pick the wrong tree?

Communication can be relative: Police got a report of an altercation in the lounge of a Waipouli hotel. It turned out to be a Kaua'i couple having a heated argument. The couple left the bar and continued their "conversation" outside. Apparently they came to "terms," or so she thought, and she went back into the bar. The man was last seen pounding his head on a tree in the parking lot.

You just can't have two wives... A report of someone getting married illegally on Kaua'i came from a woman on the mainland, who provided the Attorney General's Office in Honolulu with what she felt was proof that her husband had taken a second wife in a (no doubt lovely) wedding ceremony at the Fern Grotto, so police are investigating.

(But probably no one told her that Hawai'i is one of the few places where a second marriage without the benefit of a divorce is only a misdemeanor. A law was passed here making it a minor offense, possibly because, so often in the past, men left their home country with plans to make enough money to send for their families or return home. However, they never made it back home, so they took a second wife and had a second family.)

Valuables change with age... A woman who had a fight with her boyfriend stole his insulin and his pills for gout and high blood pressure... a woman said she and her husband had an argument, and when he stormed off, he took the four tires from her car with him... there was a report of a family fight in front of police headquarters (saving the officers time and gas)... and a Kapa'a woman complained that her husband had violated a restraining order by sending her flowers on Mother's Day.

How embarrassing... A report of a male beating up a female at the entrance to The Westin Hotel (and welcome to the land of aloha)... a woman asked police to speak to her husband about his drinking problem, but please don't tell him that she called... and a Kaumakani man told police that the things his wife told them about him were untrue.

North Shore real estate sales technique... Police were concerned that there might have been a robbery and possibly a kidnapping in Hanalei when a driver peeled out of town, chasing after a sports car.

POLICE BLOTTER

The man and woman in the sports car headed towards Hanalei Bridge. The man doing the chasing forced the sports car over to the side of the road, jumped out of his car and abandoned it in the middle of the road. He climbed into the driver's seat of the sports car, pushing the woman driver into the passenger seat and knocking the male passenger out the other side. The man then took off in the sports car with the woman.

The male passenger left standing on the side of the road was understandably puzzled and upset when the sports car sped off, not only with the real estate lady agent who had been showing him properties, but also because his camera and money were in the back seat.

As it turned out, the real estate lady had had a fight with her boyfriend, who owned the sports car, and then she had driven the sports car to work. When the boyfriend saw her zooming by with another man in his car, he took off in hot pursuit.

But everything was finally settled, with the real estate prospect getting an apology and his belongings returned, and the boyfriend getting a citation for obstructing traffic with the vehicle he abandoned in the middle of the highway.

Well, *someone* did it... Police were kind enough to give a woman who had had too much to drink a ride home, and the next morning she called to say that the police had beaten her up. She called back later and said after thinking about it, she decided it might have been her boyfriend who did the damage to her face after she arrived home drunk.

Free speech can have repercussions... A caller reported a fight on the West side, allegedly caused by one guy saying that the other guy's girlfriend looked like a "toad."

Can't we just be friends? A woman asked to speak to an officer about her "sugar daddy." She said she had forsaken her octogenarian boyfriend in favor of a "younger" man – in his 40s. But her new young boyfriend was very possessive, and she didn't want him to harm the old, old boyfriend because she was still fond of him.

Husbands take vacations... A North Shore woman reported that her husband "disappeared" two weeks ago. He left the island on Super Bowl Sunday, and he was holding all the bet money, so she feels his absence may be intentional... a Wailua woman said she hadn't seen her husband for two days, and it turned out he failed to tell her he was taking a vacation . . . and a Princeville man reported his wife, 54, as missing, but her car was found at the airport and it was learned she had made advance reservations.

Talk about a set-up: A Waimea man was charged with theft at the Kaua'i Surf Hotel when he couldn't pay for a lovely dinner for two at the Golden Cape. A woman he'd just met invited him to dinner, then after the meal, excused herself to the powder room, and never returned... and another woman had a fight with her boyfriend and pitched him and all his things, including his two rifles in their cases, out the door. Then she called police and reported that there was a man outside her house with a rifle.

A *baby*!? But... but... how could this happen? Police were called to settle matters after doctors and nurses at Wilcox Hospital had spent four hours trying to convince a man who had brought his wife to the emergency room with stomach pains that she had given birth to a baby. He obviously hadn't known she was expecting and, being unexpecting, he refused to believe he was a new father (if indeed he was the new father).

Just AWOL... two women reported not having seen their husbands for three days, but police found that both men were okay (physically if not domestically).

A trip through the canefield... A local couple who had a friend visiting from the mainland started out in the morning, drinking and sightseeing, and by 3 p.m., they were well on the way to being drunk, in a truck, in a canefield in Nawiliwili.

The woman said it was about that time that her boyfriend started arguing and wanted to fight their visiting friend. She said he gets crazy when he gets mad, and she was afraid that he would hurt her after fighting with his friend. So when the two men got out of the truck, she took off.

Then things got messy. The woman hadn't driven very far when she had trouble with the truck and had to stop. She was trying to fix something on the engine when a Lihuʻe Plantation haul cane truck came by and the driver got out to help her.

As he was trying to get the pickup started, the boyfriend came running up. He grabbed the LP driver and challenged him to fight; the driver said he had no choice but to punch him. Twice the driver let the boyfriend get up off the ground when he agreed to cool off, but each time he came at the driver again and twice more he got knocked down.

The LP driver then helped the woman get into his truck – the cab is eight feet off the ground – and they drove off together. They met his boss in the field, and the driver turned the woman over to the boss to take her back to the mill.

Meanwhile, the boyfriend had gotten the pickup started and began pursuing the boss and the woman. The boyfriend was driving crazily, so the boss radioed ahead for police.

All was *pau* by the time the cops arrived. The LP driver said, "I didn't want to fight. I don't even know the guy." The woman said, "It was all my boyfriend's fault."

The boyfriend said, "Me and my old lady just had a slight argument, then she split and left me behind." He said he ran after her, then he saw her with the LP driver. He was really mad, but added, "The driver wasted me, man, he beat the s--- out of me. I may be slightly drunk, but I can't believe what happened." The boyfriend refused medical treatment and wisely said he wasn't interested in filing charges against the LP driver.

Because the woman was too shook up to drive and the boyfriend was still too drunk, the police gave the couple a ride in a blue-and-white to the police station, where she called a friend to take them home.

It's not known if the mainland visitor is still wandering in the cane field wondering what happened and where he is.

Off the Record

There are often stories and anecdotes I hear at the police station, in court, when talking to cops and prosecutors, on the phone, or over the scanner. These don't make it onto the blotter, so they don't make it into the newspaper. But they provide a good look at the fringes and loose ends of law enforcement on the Garden Island.

Good-at-math-but-unclear-on-the-concept: When a young woman was confronted by the boss of the company she was (formerly) working for about the theft of $18,200, she readily admitted taking the money. She appeared contrite and thought a moment, and then said to him, "How about you give me another $1,800, then I'll owe you an even $20,000?"

Compulsive fill-in-the-blanks dept.: The dispatcher told a West side patrolman that there was a report of a horse galloping down the street in Kekaha Gardens subdivision. The cop asked, "Did they say which side of the street it's on or what color it is?"

POLICE BLOTTER

The *real* good ol' days: When Kaua'i got its new state-run community correctional center (i.e., the jail), an old-timer reminisced about the days when, in an earlier incarnation, the jail was known as the Montgomery Hotel (named after the jailer). Prisoners used to be allowed to go fishing during the day, and there was a sign on the door that said, "All prisoners not back by 6:30 p.m. will be locked out for the night."

And that reminded another old-timer of a time when the jail was located in Nawiliwili next to the dog pound. The prisoners put on a big lu'au for the police officers on New Year's Day, and there was considerable discussion about whether the meat they were eating was pink pig or black dog.

And that old jail, also called the Wailua Hilton, was so picturesque that, just before it was torn down, filmmakers used it for location shots for the not-very-well-known low-budget movie "Acapulco Gold."

Precision-has-no-soul... It's only been in recent years that street numbers have been used in giving a description of how to get from here to there. A not uncommon description, overheard on the police scanner, was: "Just before up the hill, by the lychee tree, by Vernon guys' house."

Back before there were helicopters... I remember, in the early 1970s, when I first started covering the "death and disaster" beat, there weren't helicopters readily available for search and rescue missions as there are today. Back then, it was Samson Mahuiki and his Ha'ena scrub ponies who made the trek up Na Pali trails to search for hikers in trouble. He had his ponies tied along Hanalei River and they were available night and day, in good weather and bad. This brave and kind Hawaiian, with his horses that could manage the rushing waters and rough terrain, provided an important service for the people of Kaua'i and their visitors.

Boy, the nerve of some guys... A disgruntled officer was saying a guy who, at one time or another, has threatened to kill probably every officer on the force, is himself being threatened, over the phone no less, and he called for police protection. Go figure!

So are you recommending hard time or leniency? A criminal, waiting for the judge to appear in Circuit Court to sentence him, said to the (then) prosecuting attorney Calvin Murashige, who had been his classmate at Kapa'a High School, "How come you come good-looking now? You was ugly in school."

Kids (and the people who make them): In a story about three juveniles who terrorized some visitors at Koke'e State Park, I chose to refer to them as "punks" because their names couldn't be used. In the story, I noted that they were detained on misdemeanor assault charges and said, "and the crummiest one of them all also faces a sexual abuse charge. They were turned over to their parents' custody (and don't you hope they have parents who don't believe in ganging up, threatening, grabbing, punching, and pulling knives... and will make that clear... somehow)."

The next day, one of the boys' mothers called me (probably the mother of the crummiest one), furious that I had recounted what happened when they were "just" juveniles. I reminded her that I hadn't used their names, had just referred to them as "punks," to which the mother replied, "Yeah, but now everyone knows who they are!"

Another example of such parents – to use the term loosely – is those who threatened a woman after police arrested their kids for burglarizing her home.

"Then think what a great guy he'll be in 6 months."

Ya gotta be fast on your feet: A defense attorney was asking that his client be released from jail after he'd served just three months' time. He said the client had matured, become responsible, developed a proper attitude, and so on. The prosecutor replied that if three months had been such a help to him, think of what a great guy he'd be in six months. The judge agreed with the prosecutor and denied the defendant's motion for sentence reduction.

Unofficial police department policy: Given the fact that this is such a small island that you can't hide, and given the fact that you can't even get off it after 8:30 p.m. when the last flight leaves Lihu'e Airport, after police were involved in a high-speed chase, I asked then-Sgt. Bernard Naea if there was a policy about hot pursuit. "Sure there is. If you're a young cop you chase 'em, and if you're an old cop, you don't," Ber said.

Holoholona (animals)

There are animals (creatures and fowls) that Kaua'i has and doesn't have, that make it somewhat different from other places. There are also differing attitudes here about these animals because this is a multicultural community and because problems arise as neighborhoods sprout up in what were rural areas.

The "live and let live" attitude is changing, but except for the mainly *malihini* (newcomer) subdivisions in Princeville and Po'ipu, Kauaians in most areas still live close to animals, if not within sight, certainly within hearing or smelling distance.

Pigs and goats... On Na Pali Coast, goats run wild and there are wild pigs that have truly fearsome tusks and ugly dispositions and occasionally come down from the mountains and into town. Europeans and Americans imported them for hunting, and while they are good for that purpose, they are also causing serious erosion and decimation of native plants and animals along the rugged coast and in the valleys along the pali.

Donkeys... There are a few mules left over from the days when they were used on the plantations. Sometimes they are taken by hunters for packing when they go up on the treacherous Na Pali to hunt pig and goat, and you can occasionally see local people riding mules as if they were horses.

Lucky we don't have... There are no snakes here and only Kaua'i has no mongoose. Poisonous spiders aren't a problem, although there are ugly ol' centipedes that can deliver a nasty bite.

Tiny lizards... Geckos abound. They are a part of almost every household: They lay their eggs nestled into crevices, their tongues lap at the jelly knife on the kitchen counter, they gather around the porch lights to gobble down bugs. They can be delightful to watch – but their droppings are everywhere.

Beware of man-o-war... The proximity of the ocean means that creatures from the sea make the news occasionally. Those pesky Portuguese man-o-war jellyfish that look like blue plastic bubbles wash ashore on the east side throughout the trade winds season (spring through fall), and they can sting both in and out of the water.

And although they're usually encountered only when spear-fishing, the evil-looking and biting eels should definitely be avoided.

Seals are protected... Hawaiian monk seals, which come ashore to sleep, are fascinating, but getting near one is prohibited because they are an endangered species. However, 56 of the total estimated population of about 1500 regularly ply the waters of the main islands, including Kaua'i. If you see one, just keep your distance and let it rest.

POLICE BLOTTER

Yes, Virginia, there are sharks... Over the years sharks have occasionally attacked swimmers, surfers and divers, but I can only recall two people being killed by sharks off Kaua'i. Many years ago, a local fishing boat sank in the 15-mile-wide Kaulakahi Channel between Kaua'i and Ni'ihau. The men swam all night through the shark-infested waters until they washed up on the beach – and the sharks never touched them.

Local men who dive and spear fish and squid don't seem to worry about them. When they spot a shark, they might poke it on the nose with the spear, then slowly back away, but they never, ever, take their eyes off it. For some Hawaiians, the shark is their *'aumakua* (family or personal god), a special relationship that is never discussed.

"What's an estray Bovine?"

Dispatch: "It's a cow out for a stroll."

A whole bunch of cows... A lot of people are surprised to discover that Hawai'i has many cattle (always called cows in Hawai'i, regardless of sex) and the *paniolos* (cowboys) to take care of them. There is also still some cattle rustling. The number of cattle is dwindling as the price of land goes up and ranchers can't afford to pay taxes on property big enough to pasture the animals.

Keeping fences mended presents a problem, and if the cows get out, that presents more problems. Finding the owner isn't always easy – it has been said that no one owns cows after 9 o'clock at night, when dispatchers are trying to find someone to round up those "estray bovines." The cows are also likely to get on the highway and get hit and there's been more than one lawsuit for injuries (to motorists) in those cases.

Too many to count... There are countless dogs and cats, owned and strays – feral domestic cats are a primary predator of endangered Hawaiian birds and other animals. Kaua'i still has strong rural customs, and there are often differences between people who are used to house pets and those who, for example, use dogs for hunting only and the rest of the time keep them caged or tied up in the backyard.

Getting the pig ready... The idea of killing and gutting a pig at one's house to get it ready for the *imu* for a *lu'au* also upsets newcomers who aren't used to this sort of thing.

There are the chickens, everywhere... Some are raised to be fighting chickens and are well cared for, trained and very valuable. The idea of their fighting, armed with gaffs, upsets some people, but gambling on the chicken fights has been such a big part of life for many people here, for so long, the police can only try to "keep it down and keep it local."

Most of the chickens you see now, though, are wild. Some people like them, get used to the crowing and just tune it out. But believe me, there's no such thing as them crowing just "at the break of day." Some people find them pesky and worry about mites. One person will do everything possible to drive them away from his house while a neighbor next door feeds them. But friend or foe, it's hard not to smile as you stop to wait for the mother hen to herd her chicks across the road.

From the Daily Blotter: There are oodles of reports of "estrays" all around the island every week, but a call from Rosemarie Newsome of Waimea, saying that there was a strange horse in her garage, seemed worthy of note... a Kapaʻa woman called to report that there was a swine at her home damaging her property... a Hanamaʻulu woman said there was a pig at her house... and a Hanapepe caller said there was a jackass in his yard fooling around with his horse.

Drunken horse and cowboy... A late-night caller said a drunken cowboy on a horse, which looked like it had had a few beers also, were creating a disturbance in Hanalei town... a Puhi woman reported finding a pair of boy's underpants and a stepladder in her cow pasture... and Vernon White of Anahola reported finding 12 cow legs on ʻAliomanu Road.

Dog sandwich??? A caller said a construction worker was eating a dog sandwich, but a police officer who checked the worker's lunch box called back to say it looked like baloney to him... a stray kitten that had been hanging around the Health Department building in Lihuʻe was found skinned, with its paws missing, lying on the ground outside a psychiatrist's office (loaded with implications)… and police were called to remove the head of a cow from the driveway of a doctor's office in Kapaʻa.

A horse is charged with rape… Two west side families have been feuding for years, like the Hatfields and McCoys, and it led to an interesting courtroom battle. One evening the stallion of one family visited the mare of the other family and there was a noisy interlude. The mare's owner then took the stallion's family to court seeking damages for the "rape" of their animal.

The stallion was not branded, so the owner's lawyer, while cross-examining the plaintiff's expert witness, Tony Wong, asked, "How do you know it was my client's horse?" Tony, unmoved by such a question, asked the lawyer how many children he had. The lawyer replied that he had three. Tony then asked, "How many are branded?" The creative and resilient lawyer quickly cross-claimed for "stud fees."

Just taking a snooze… There was a report of a bull napping on nice warm Kuhio Highway pavement on the North Shore. The big boy belonged to Doc Johnston of Princeville Ranch, and police were asked to remove it. It wasn't easy, but they were finally able to convince him to find a less inconvenient place to snooze.

Need to know bovine traits… Near the big concrete bridge as you head toward the North Shore, there's a pasture that abuts the Kalihiwai Stream and is fenced on the other three sides. One of the cows pastured there decided to explore and found herself in the middle of the bridge in the middle of the night. An unsuspecting motorist was unable to stop in time to avoid colliding with the bovine.

A lawsuit was filed. The insurance company's defense lawyer, a Honolulu city boy, claimed the pasture owner was not negligent because he could not have anticipated that the cow could swim across the stream. Cows can't swim, he declared as his answer to the complaint.

The plaintiff's lawyer, also unfamiliar with bovine traits, decided to ask Public Defender Jim Jung what he knew about cows. Jung suggested he buy a copy of Disney's "Castaway Cowboy," which was filmed just up the road from the scene of the accident, near Moloaʻa Bay.

It showed how the cowboys got their cattle aboard a ship. The animals swam from the beach, then they were hauled aboard in slings. "And if you look closely at the cowboy 'extras' in the film, you can see what the pasture's owner looked like when he was a few years younger," Jung said.

The Public Defender said the case was settled on the issue of liability before it went to trial. The insurance company lawyer didn't want to be embarrassed with his theory of defense before a Kauaʻi jury.

And that reminds me... One poor cow that wandered onto Kuhio Hwy. got hit by three different cars in one evening. But after the dispatcher made all the calls to all the ranchers on her list and none of them claimed ownership, a rancher who is not known especially for his civic spirit went out and hauled that cow away at 1 a.m. and buried it some place. He said the next day that he'd done it for health reasons, adding, "You can't just leave a dead cow on the road." General suspicion, however, was that it was probably branded, the brand was probably that rancher's, and he was trying to insure that he wasn't named as the defendant in three lawsuits.

So what's the problem? There was a complaint about some dead ducks in the back of a pickup truck, but no one could figure out what was wrong with having dead ducks in the back of a pickup... a woman asked to speak to an officer about her "fowls"... a cow fell off a cliff on the North Shore... and a caller asked police to remove some cows from a prawn pond.

Don't disturb Mother Nature... A report of a beached whale in Ha'ena brought a marine mammals expert from Honolulu. It wasn't easy but a boat was used to drag the false killer whale back out to sea. The big fellow wasn't going to be deterred from his mission though, and he came right back to shore. He was given a physical examination and when it was determined that he had what appeared to be a fatal case of pneumonia, he was given a lethal injection to shorten the period of suffering.

A ram on a rampage... Ralph Shrinski of Puhi told police that a goat rammed his vehicle, causing extensive damages... two "estray" bovines were reported to be headed for saimin at Hamura's in downtown Lihu'e after dark one night... a man said someone else's horse beat up his horse (and the police are supposed to do something about that?)... and there was an estray pig (the four-legged kine) headed for Tahiti Nui in Hanalei.

Wow, a snake, here?... A Lawa'i man's report that he was about to retrieve a snake from his swimming pool caused a lot of excitement, but the magnification on his face mask must have caused it to look more threatening than it was, because it turned out to be a 4-5-inch earthworm... and Marie Wilson reported two monkeys loose in her yard.

POLICE BLOTTER

"You gotta wait for the estrays."

I'd squeal too, wouldn't you... When police investigated a call about a pig squealing in Kealia, they found the pig was squealing for good reason - he was about to go into the *imu* and come out as *kalua*... someone called to say that the extra cow in his pasture should be removed before it gets slaughtered ... and a horse fell into the swimming pool at the old Kaua'i Inn. (auwe!)

A dog stuck with a pot... A caller in Anahola asked for police to help with a dog with a pot stuck on its head, but by the time police arrived, either the dog had gotten the pot off its head or it had run away with the pot still on its head because police couldn't find a dog with a pot on its head (whew!).

Dead dolphin... There was a report of a dead baby dolphin washed up on the beach at Kealia. Department of Land and

Natural Resources ranger Nolan Rapozo said it was a newborn, about two feet long, and because it was partially decomposed, he just took it to the dump. If it had been in good shape, he said, he would have put it in a freezer and then sent it to Oʻahu for an autopsy and research.

Be sure to look a "gift horse" in the mouth... Jurgen Sharpe of Kapaʻa found a horse and was unsuccessful in finding the owner, so he decided to keep it. That was until a vet took a look at it, checked the mouth and said the horse was mighty old and very tired.

With it being so much trouble to get rid of a dead horse (by burning it for days or digging a very large grave), Jurgen decided it would be best to relinquish ownership before its imminent demise. Officials at the Humane Society kindly agreed to accept it, but the tired old horse is still tied up (in red tape) until they can find a county vehicle that can transport it to the shelter in Hanapepe.

Turtle nappers nabbed: Following up on a tip that there were two live green sea turtles in the bed of a pickup truck at Ahukini, officers found the turtles and the men responsible for taking the endangered animals. Police photographed the turtles and then, because the turtles looked healthy enough to survive, returned them to the ocean. The officers also reported the incident to the Department of Land and Natural Resources, which in turn notified the National Marine Fisheries division in Honolulu. The maximum penalty for violations of the federal Native Species Act is a $50,000 fine and a year in jail.

Pursuit of the chicken fighters... The chicken fights planned for last Sunday were postponed indefinitely following a round-the-island chase. Police said off-island gamblers arrived here that Sunday morning, and with 18 rental cars jammed with people and chickens, headed for "the only game in town" – the well-known arena on Kahuna Road in Kapahi.

It was the only game in town because it was molting season – owners don't let the chickens fight when they're losing their feathers. The off-island chicken fighters brought birds imported from the mainland, where the molting season is different, and this offered local gamblers their only chance to bet on the chickens. (Kauaʻi's gamblers don't import birds because they cost as much as $400 each, and not many local people can afford them at that price.)

"We chased them from Kahuna Road all the way over to Kalaheo and then out to Kekaha," vice officer Bobby Castro said. "They finally gave up, and we saw them off at the airport at 3 p.m. They were really mad, but we told them that if they want to have a circus, have a circus on your own island."

"Aloha also means goodbye."

Chicken scratch... A note on the Police Blotter said "a woman would like to speak to an officer about her rash." After we stopped laughing, we discovered that she really does have a problem. Wild chickens are roaming around under her house, and she believes the rash was caused by the mites that chickens carry around. What she really wanted to ask the officer was how to get rid of the unwanted chickens.

Don't fool with the roaster... Another item on the Blotter attracted our attention because it noted a woman reported that the neighbor children were molesting her "roaster." As it turned out, the kids were mistreating her rooster, so police talked to the kids' father, who assured them he would handle the problem.

And one more chicken item: On Mother's Day, a police officer went to put flowers on his mother's grave in Koloa and discovered chicken fights were being held in the cemetery.

Not a slippery-kine eel... Longtime fisherman-diver Dallas Grady of Kilauea had a nasty encounter with a five-foot-long, 15-pound *puhi paka* moray eel that grabbed his thigh and mangled his hand before it finally let go.

Dallas and his brother were pole fishing at Pila'a. At his waist, Dallas had tied a nylon bag for fish he had already caught. He was hooking near the channel, knee-deep in the water, when he felt something grab onto his inner thigh. It was a yellow and brown moray, a large, strong, fierce eel armed with a nightmarish, gaping mouthful of needle-sharp teeth. The eel was going after the fish in Dallas's bag. He reached for the eel, but it grabbed onto his hand, and he had to wrestle with it before it released him.

He had surgery at Wilcox Hospital, then went to an orthopedic hand specialist in Honolulu who had to amputate Grady's ring finger and performed plastic surgery on another finger; his other fingers and his leg were expected to heal. Dallas bore no anger toward the eel, which he said was just following its instincts, and added, "It's a reminder that you have to be careful and respectful of the ocean and its creatures."

Only on Kaua'i: Police got a call about a loose pig running through a yard on Akemama Road in Lawa'i. Kaua'i being the kind of place it is – neighborly and pig-oriented – someone in the neighborhood knew how to lasso a pig and did so. The next problem was: What do we do with this pig? No one knew who owned it.

Another well-intentioned neighbor offered to take it home and eat it; the police lieutenant on the scene nixed that idea and tried unsuccessfully to get in touch with the Humane Society. Another neighbor then suggested that a police officer who lives in the area and who raises pigs might be willing to keep it. Finally, when all seemed lost, along came someone who, wouldn't you know it, recognized the pig!

Geckos on Radiation... Of course we have our iguana stories. Possession of iguanas is illegal in Hawai'i, but prior to the latest "find" in Kilauea, state officials had captured three on Kaua'i.

In the early 1980s, two fishermen spotted a big, three-to-four-foot-long iguana in Moloa'a and captured it by throwing a net over it.

In 1989, two kids had a three-footer in their car in Hanama'ulu. There was a high-speed chase to 'Oma'o (the iguana was the lookout), and when police finally stopped the kids, they refused to hand over the iguana. Only when the police threatened to impound their car did the kids surrender the hot lizard.

And in 1991, three men saw an iguana run across Kaumualiʻi Highway as they were driving through Lawaʻi. They bailed out of the car and gave chase, but the iguana fled up a 30-foot embankment on the roadside. Police and a staffer at the Pacific Tropical Botanical Gardens managed to catch the two-and-one-half-foot-long reptile, which an Agriculture Department quarantine inspector took to send off to the Honolulu Zoo.

Kauaʻi "cowabunga"... A calf-roping event planned for the Sunday rodeo at Kealia got started earlier than anticipated when some of the Princeville Cattle Company's young cows managed to break loose as they were being unloaded at the arena. The newly-freed calves raced off in all directions, and soon rope-swinging cowboys began giving chase on horseback and in pickup trucks.

The unplanned roundup netted a few calves headed toward Anahola and some racing in the opposite direction down Kuhio Highway toward Kapaʻa town. But several of the cows remained elusive, and the pursuit was hampered by the noise and confusion of the mountain ball tournament being played at the Kapaʻa ball park.

Princeville's Mike Longley said he saw one of the calves running into the ocean, and while he was chasing yet another calf, the ocean-going calf got back to shore and was roped as he raced around the Kapaʻa Library.

Another calf then ran into the ocean near the ball park, and hundreds of spectators gathered as cowboys raced their horses along the water's edge, trying to rope the calf as it floundered

POLICE BLOTTER 71

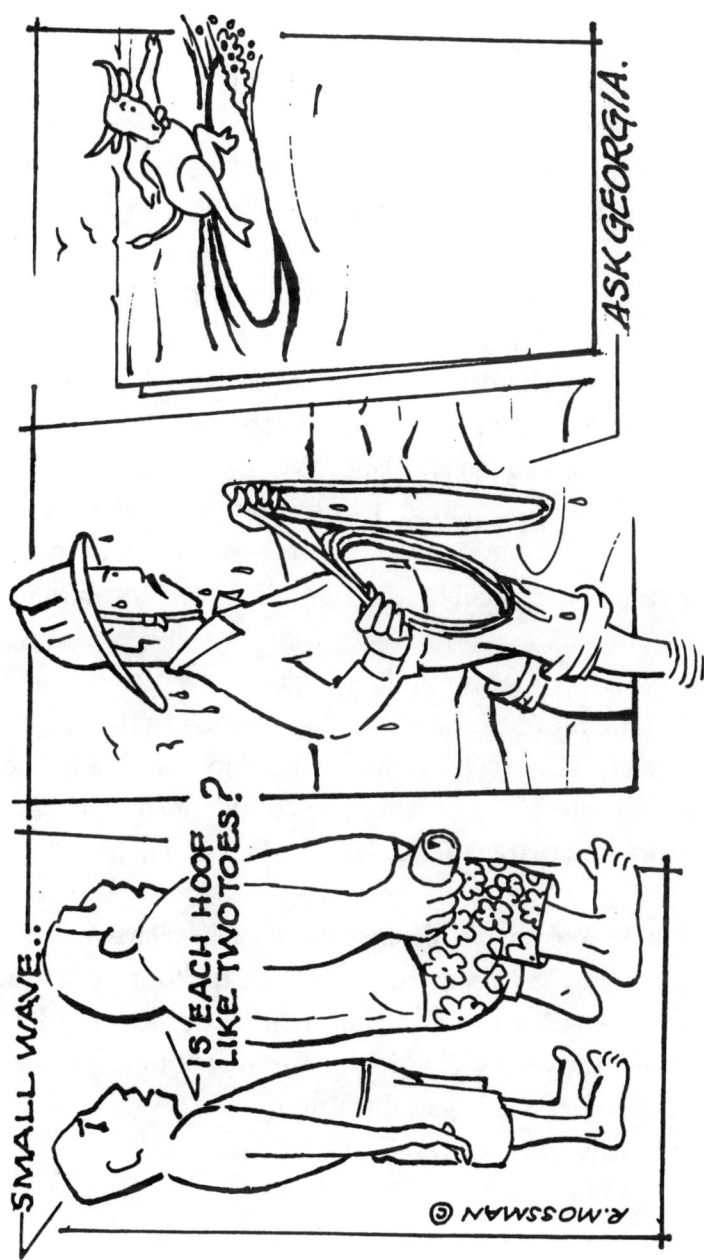

Better a ride than a rodeo The estray took to the

on the reef some 50 feet offshore. Someone called the fire department, and the Kapaʻa firemen raced to the scene, then joined the spectators and sat atop their big red truck.

By now the entire community was involved: cowboys, firemen, police, baseball players, fans, librarians, tourists. Longley said he realized they weren't going to be able to save the calf while on horseback, so he borrowed the fire department's big rescue surfboard and made his way out to the terrified young cow. He wrestled a rope around the calf and kept it from drowning by holding its head up on the board as the animal kicked and he paddled. Everyone cheered when the drenched cowboy and the scared calf made it safely back to shore.

Longley said they figured that the poor calf had had enough exercise, so they took him back to the arena and let him spend the day resting and recuperating, and the rodeo got started only half an hour late.

He didn't realize until later that three calves were still missing. One more calf was found at about 11 p.m. Sunday in Butchie Victorino's pasture and returned to its mother. The last two are still missing, so if you see a couple of strange calves in your pasture (or garage), please give Mike a call.

You're Invited to the Hammerheads' Baby Shower... It was just like the movies. As in "Jaws". At Kalapaki Bay one August Sunday in 1994, in front of what is now the Kauaʻi Marriott Hotel, someone yelled "SHARK!" Everyone bounded out of the water, and onlookers began screaming.

It was truly scary for David and Christina Cole, who were in a 14-foot ski boat in the middle of the bay. It was even scarier for Jake Camp, who was on a surfboard nearby, feet dangling deliciously down.

The Coles saw five or six hammerhead sharks, each about

15 feet long, circling the area. Camp paddled frantically to reach their boat as people started screaming "SWIM! SWIM!" One shark began swirling around and heading for Camp, and then began to give birth to a bunch of babies - a big bunch of big babies. First there were five or six hammerheads; then there were dozens of hammerheads.

Managing to grab Camp, the Coles hauled him into the boat as the shark approached the rear of the boat, dove under it and came up out of the water in front of it. The water in that area is no more than 10 feet deep at high tide. The shark was so big, it created a wave that swamped the boat's engine. Afraid that the boat was going to sink, the trio began bailing frantically so they could try to start the engine. It started and they made it to shore, but it was a harrowing experience. David Cole said it gives him chicken skin to even think about it.

Our local shark expert, state aquatic biologist Don Heacock said it's not unusual for hammerheads to come into sheltered areas like Kalapaki to give birth. The mother hammerhead thrashes around, lifting its dorsal and tail fins out of the water, and delivers from 20 to 40 "pups," each 18 to 20 inches long, complete with sharp little teeth. The sheltered bay serves as both a nursery and, with its schools of small fish, a feeding ground for the babies.

"When you see a shark that size," Heacock said, "it's prudent to get out of the water because occasionally the unpredictable happens, even though hammerheads have never been implicated in shark attacks in Hawai'i."

Everybody's baby monk seal... A monk seal gave birth to a pup on the North Shore a few years ago. The mother stayed with her baby for almost six months, to feed her and and teach her until she was old enough to fend for herself.

Over 200 volunteers from the Haʻena community were concerned about the mother and baby and protected them from intrusion around the clock. When the pup became so fat she could survive if necessary for several months without food, the mother seal swam away.

But the baby was – in the words of state aquatic biologist Don Heacock – like a big "aquatic Labrador puppy," with no fear of humans and wanting to play. A storm blew her down to Keʻe Beach at the northern end of Na Pali coast. State officials then decided to take her away from the area where she had so many friends, and trucked her to the south shore. But again, she kept popping up, on boogie boards, at popular swimming beaches looking for friends and even at picnic lunches.

Fishery officials decided that was too dangerous for her, so to prevent her from consorting with friends and strangers, they used a boat to tow her the 20 miles to Niʻihau. She had been tagged, but she hasn't been seen now for several years.

'Aihue
(Thief; to steal)
What's Mine is Yours . . . and Especially Vice-Versa

Although Kaua'i and Hawai'i are relatively safe as far as violent crimes are concerned, the statistics on the number of thefts place the state in the top five in the country for property crimes.

It may play only a small role in accounting for the number of thefts, but there is a different sense of property here. For example, the Hawaiian concept of "what's mine is yours" is wonderful. By the same token, the accompanying, "what's yours is mine," requires a major shift in attitude for newcomers.

There's also the "I like borrow…" approach, often with no malice intended, but also with no definite plan for returning the item. And that's coupled with an attitude about things that are missing, which is, "Eh, it got legs."

Then too, the entire state is a tourist destination, and visitors often get too relaxed and don't take any precautions when they're vacationing. Add to that, the growing need of some people here to support a drug habit, and that's at least a partial explanation for too many car break-ins and thefts.

Lu'au to broke da mouf? For some unknown reason, someone broke into Akutagawa's Market in Kapa'a and stole 12 bags – 550 pounds – of rice… a burglar hit Fairway Restaurant at the

Wailua Golf Course and made off with plenny ono grines: a case of tuna, a case of corned beef, and a case and a half of Spam (had to be a local thief: only Kauaians would consider Spam worth stealing)... Not to be outdone, a seafood lover broke into the Sea Shell Restaurant and scooped up four pounds of scallops, four pounds of shrimp, four pounds of prawns, 20 pounds of lobster tails, and 10 pieces of sliced mahi mahi... another lobster-tail lover helped himself to a whole case of them from JJ's Broiler... yet another thief with a big appetite burgled Kealia Store for 15 dozen eggs and 25 cases of Oly. (These food sources were the precursors to what is now known as a "party store.")

I love my poi... Someone stole two bags of taro (again, a purely local-style appetite) from Carol Haraguchi's Hanalei fields, but at least they were considerate enough to pick their own and not steal the taro already bagged... a finger-lickin' thief stole four bags of Kentucky Fried Chicken... a thirsty thief stole seven cases of chocolate milk at Waimea High School... and a burglar with a sweet tooth broke into a Wailua home and stole money and a pumpkin pie.

Don't forget the end tables... Apparently someone who has a yen for wicker furniture and no qualms about stealing helped himself to three white wicker chairs from Plantation Gardens in Poʻipu. Two nights later, someone took four more chairs and two wicker tables from the same restaurant. And there was also a report of a lovely, large queen's wicker chair "disappearing" from Kiahuna, right near Plantation Gardens.

Who Owns Your Medical Records? A patient at Wilcox Hospital asked a records clerk to make copies of his medical file. As the staffer was trying to figure out what portions he needed, the patient grabbed the entire file and left. Then came a call reporting a theft at the hospital. But the officer was faced with the problems of trying to decide: Just who really "owns" the file? And would he be violating the patient's right to privacy if he looked at the file to verify whose it was?

The patient went to the police station a couple of days later and rather dramatically tried to turn himself in, but the officer still hadn't decided if it really was a crime. (More of life's perplexing problems.)

Unconfirmed but heartwarming report... Reportedly two local punks, well-known to police, attempted to hold up a Japanese tourist couple at knife-point in Waipouli. It turned out the male tourist was a karate expert and gave the local thugs a dirty licking. (We don't usually deal in unconfirmed reports but the possibility warmed our hearts.)

Go Figure... A Canadian visitor reported the theft of a top coat, a suit, shoes, and liquor from his Waipouli hotel room. (The booze, maybe, but why would anyone want a top coat, suit and shoes HERE?)... and a woman reported that her husband went to pick up the washing machine she had left at her old house in Kealia but returned with the wrong washing machine, leading to the discovery that someone had made a "trade-in" for her newer model.

It's-a-Very-Small-Island... A Puhi man was charged with theft when someone recognized the two batiks hanging on his wall as those that were missing from the wall at Po'ipu Inn... and police charged a young Kapa'a man with burglary after a hotel guest spotted him wearing clothes that had belonged to the guest prior to the burglary of his room.

Who He? A late-night caller told police that he was the assistant manager at GEMs in Lihuʻe. He said there were two people near the store's front door, and he was afraid they were trying to break in. Police checked, found no one there and no signs of attempts to enter the building. When they called the manager to report their findings, he said he was glad that the store hadn't been burglarized, but on the other hand, he'd never heard of the person who had said he was the assistant manager (???).

But boss, the passengers wanted me to wait! Police got a 4 a.m. report that a 15-passenger taxi had been stolen from a Nawiliwili nightclub parking lot. They discovered that the cab owner drove into town after hearing that his driver had been using the van to go nightclubbing after work, picked up the van ,and drove it home. When the driver called the owner to tell him the cab had been stolen, the owner told him he was fired.

Stealing home... When some tenants returned home and discovered their back porch and half the bedroom floor was gone, they called police. It turned out that their landlord, thinking they had already moved out, had started some renovations; he put them up in a hotel for the night.

In the "I Wonder Why" Category: And the winners are: whoever burgled the Grove Farm's rock-crushing plant and the maid's closet at Islander Inn.

"Those panty hose. They're you."

This is your brain on drugs... A man deprived of a drug he was hooked on went to a local pharmacy and asked what time it closed. When he learned he had a little time, he went to a nearby store and purchased a pair of panty hose and a water pistol. He pulled the panty hose over his head – but not over his face – and with the legs flopping like the ears of an elderly rabbit, he hopped back to the pharmacy, pointed the pistol at the pharmacist, and said, "Give me your drugs."

The pharmacist, not knowing whether to laugh or cry, suggested he take a seat. The would-be robber was still trying to figure out what had gone wrong with the heist as the local gendarmes took him away.

Off the Record, Again

Honest Sarge, she got the drop on me! At the police department, I overheard that a patrolman working the night shift invited a young woman he'd met to join him in the backseat of his patrol car for an intimate "discussion," and they'd both gotten in the car quickly and closed the doors.

Oops! The back doors automatically lock, there are no handles on the inside, and it was a cage car – a heavy-duty fence keeps the backseat passenger (usually a prisoner) from getting into the front seat.

You wonder if they were able to relax and enjoy their "discussion," knowing that the only way they were going to get out of that car was to be discovered together in the backseat of the blue-and-white. And with the officer unable to respond to radio calls, he knew it wouldn't be long before several officers, including his sergeant, would be arriving to make sure he wasn't in trouble.

But of course, this is just an unconfirmed rumor.

Threatened with the "Blotter"... I got a call from a woman who said she and her husband had gotten into a fight, which had gotten out of hand, and she had called the police. The officers calmed things down but didn't make an arrest.

She said her husband was now sweating it out, wondúering if his name would be in the newspaper. She had told him that if it is, she would cut it out and paste it on the bathroom mirror. I assured her that if there had been no arrest, his name wouldn't be listed on the Blotter. She paused, then said she thought she'd hold off telling him that for a few days.

Direct quote: The Daily Bulletin contained a report of a vehicle in Kapaʻa being driven in an "erotic" manner.

"I'll do *anything* !" Because I print the name of every person arrested with no exceptions, over the years there have been some very, very unhappy people when I said I couldn't accept their threat, their "bribe" (veiled and not so veiled), or their sad story. And I wish I had a nickel for everyone who said I'd hear from his lawyer, as if they all kept attorneys on retainer. Nothing, though, has ever gone beyond the talk, tears or threat stages.

Was it the cook? With the increase in population, there are more and more people with the same last name, so we have to try to be as specific as possible. For example, William Butler, Jr., of Kilauea would like it known that he is not the William Butler of Princeville who was arrested: "I'm not the Butler who did it!" he said.

Sibling rivalry: One weekly Blotter listing included the name of a West side man, 21, facing a misdemeanor marijuana charge. The young man called me and politely said that he hadn't been arrested. I checked with the police and prosecutor, and they said, yes, he had been arrested.

A little while later I listed the results of the man's appearance in court, and again he called me and said it wasn't him. So once again I checked, and this time I learned that he was right.

It was actually his 18-year-old brother who had been arrested. The younger brother was so scared that he had given the police his brother's name and age. Then it became a matter of getting the older brother "un-arrested" and "un-sentenced," and arranging for the younger brother to face the music.

Appearances count… When I look in my rear view mirror, if the driver behind me has on a white shirt and a tie, I'm sure he is an attorney who has a court appearance that day. The only other reason for the white shirt would be if he is a member of the Latter Day Saints Church on a mission.

Brought in for booking… I've seen some people who are still in a state of shock, still trying to absorb the fact that in what seems like the length of time it can take to snap your fingers, they became a "criminal."

The point is he got good representation: An attorney found a plastic bag containing a white powder in the courtroom, apparently left behind by his client, whom he'd just successfully defended on a cocaine charge.

A High-Speed Chase and the Cops Who Couldn't Shoot Straight

It was a pleasant Wednesday afternoon in October 1974. Nothing much going on. That's the way it was on Kauaʻi then. People didn't even know their own street addresses. We left our keys in the ignition and our front doors unlocked. We still put "Mr." before a suspect's name. Cops didn't have much to do. Hitchhikers were still a trusting bunch. Not much traffic. But as you'll see, there was always someone we could depend on to wake things up. The "coconut wireless" was the source of most information, but not for attribution. And that's what I had to rely on, in order to piece together this story.

A preliminary hearing was held Friday for James F. Blackwood, 25, of California and Hanalei, charged with auto theft and two counts of criminal property damage. Mr. Blackwood allegedly stole a truck from the cargo loading area at the Lihuʻe Airport and led the police on a wild "cops and robbers" chase halfway around the island.

The story, as told by a variety of eyewitnesses, *apparently* unfolded like this: Shortly after 3 p.m., police received a report of a truck being stolen from the airport and an APB was sent out to watch for the vehicle, which might be headed for the North Shore.

Anticipating that they might be able to stop a pickup truck if it came their way, Patrolman Thomas Sheldon moved in from his Kapaʻa beat to Wailua, and stationed himself across from the county jail to watch for the stolen vehicle, while Officer William Kaʻauwai moved in from his Kealia beat to the entrance at Lydgate Park. When Officer Sheldon saw the vehicle pass, he radioed ahead (gulping, we'd guess) that it wasn't a pickup truck but a 3/4-ton flatbed, coming at top speed, with the driver swerving on the highway.

It was obvious to the two men then that they weren't going to be able to stop the truck, so Kaʻauwai pulled out ahead of the truck and, with blue bar lights flashing and the siren blaring, did his best to keep the truck from passing him and to warn unsuspecting motorists to clear out of the way. With Officer Kaʻauwai in the lead, the stolen truck in the middle, and Patrolman Sheldon right behind, in the midst of heavy traffic, the police radios were abuzz with plans for trying to stop the big truck without endangering others on the highway.

Sgt. Les Kubo, officer in charge of the afternoon shift, left the Lihuʻe station to join his men, adding a third blue-and-white to the chase, and three vice officers working in the North Shore area in an unmarked car were alerted to the situation and headed toward the pursuit. The truck and its heedless driver managed to swerve in and around two police cars set up to block him at Moloaʻa, and to avoid having his tires punctured by shots fired by one of the officers there.

Unaware of the chase rapidly approaching him, Hanalei beat officer Richard Koerte was standing in the middle of the highway, busy trying to handle the mess created by 67 gallons of paint that had spilled on the highway near Princeville. He heard the sirens, looked up… and there was the flatbed bearing down on him, his car, the paint truck, and assorted onlookers. Somehow, the truck driver managed to zig-zag his way through the paint and the people there, while the police proceeded with caution, trying to avoid any unnecessary injuries.

The truck driver foiled the police when they tried to set up another roadblock at the Hanalei Bridge, and Blackwood managed to get far enough ahead of his pursuers that he had the time to stop and pick up a hitchhiker along Kuhio Highway. A short time later, he stopped to let out the hitchhiker, who was probably greatly relieved to get out of the truck being driven erratically and pursued by police cars with sirens going full blast.

The truck continued in and through Hanalei town and around all those curves, only to encounter the unmarked vice-police car completely blocking the road at Waikoko. So the truck driver swerved, crashing through a fence into a pasture (near Kaipo Chandler's place). The police continued in hot pursuit, firing at the truck careening around the pasture (with Loki Harada stopped at the bridge and frightened to death with all that was going on around her.)

The four-wheel-drive truck managed to keep going, turned around in the pasture and started heading back toward Hanalei town.

Working their way back through the crowds that had gathered along Kuhio Highway as word of the chase spread quickly, and with the crowds yelling "get 'em – shoot to kill!", the truck driver stopped once again to pick up a hitchhiker, this time in front of Laka's Gardens.

One officer said he tried to wave a warning to the fellow hitchhiking, but the fellow just waved a friendly greeting back at him, and the police were stymied once again, with orders to "proceed with caution" to avoid injury to the innocent passenger in the truck. A few minutes later, the hitchhiker got out of the truck, and as the pursuing officer passed, the hitchhiker pointed to the truck, then to his head and made a circular motion, and the pursuit continued.

The driver avoided still another roadblock, just past Hanalei Bridge, but (as we heard it) vice officer Pat Layosa, who had gotten out of the unmarked vice patrol car and into Sgt. Kubo's blue-and-white (sometime during the chase), was standing beside the road and shot point-blank at the truck tires as the driver passed through the road block. But he was using an old M-1 rifle and the bullets went into the tires, but didn't puncture them.

When the fugitive swerved to avoid the roadblock, he took off through pasture land and continued driving toward the ocean, but somewhere near Princeville, the bullet-laden engine and two tires finally gave out, and the truck came to a halt. The driver got out of the truck and surrendered peacefully. He was then escorted to the county jail where he was held in lieu of $1,000 bail.

Fortunately, and miraculously, no one was injured – and it's easy to look at the whole incident as something out of a Keystone Kops comedy, but… it points out that our officers need to be appropriately armed, with effective guns and matching ammunition… that we need a firing range so, if necessary, the officers will have practiced so they can shoot straight… and there needs to be at least a general department policy on when it's worth the risk to everyone to pursue a suspect, and when they can try to block the fugitive's "escape" by guarding the airport and hope no one will be harmed in the meantime.

'Uhane Lilo (Lost Souls)...

Kaua'i has long had its unique citizens and visitors – people who marched to a different drummer, heard a singular call, saw a vision unseen by others. Many of them become well-known to police and the community; others seem to pop up out of nowhere when the stresses and strains of life temporarily overwhelm them. The KPD's handling of these 'uhane lilo reflects the basic gentleness and tolerance of the Kaua'i kaiaulu po'e (community).

From the Daily Blotter: Police were called when a drunk wandered into a party at the Convention Hall – and they discovered he not only didn't know where he was, he didn't know who he was… a man sitting in the middle of Hassard Road told police he was just "gazing at the stars," so officers asked him to move to the side of the road and gaze at the stars from there… and someone called to say a person was driving around Hanalei town on four flat tires (maybe one of the local space cadets at the wheel?).

Direct from the drip… Police went to investigate a report that one patient had stolen drugs from another patient at Wilcox

Hospital and discovered a woman who was legitimately receiving morphine in an IV drip, who said a man came in, unhooked the tubing, used a syringe to take some of her morphine, then left.

It turned out to be the patient in the room next door and he readily admitted the theft. He said he used to use it and really liked it, so he decided to help himself. Nurses said the thief had had a foot infection and he was really well enough to leave, but he was homeless, so they'd decided to let him stay an extra day or so to give the foot a better chance of healing. With that, the patrolman told the man that he'd provide him with a place to stay and took him off to jail.

Because-it-feels-so-good-when-I-stop: An officer checked on a report that a man who attempted suicide was admitted to Wilcox Hospital. He found the patient cheerful, sitting up in bed, with a screwdriver sticking out of his stomach. The patient said it wasn't the first time he'd done this, and that he doesn't know why he does it (maybe he has a screw loose?). Orderlies then wheeled him down to surgery for removal of the screwdriver.

The Salvation Sheraton: Police kindly agreed to escort an inebriated woman from one hotel to another. But a short time later, the manager of the second hotel called to say that she wasn't a guest there and that she was running through the halls knocking on everybody's door. So police gave her a second ride, this time to the (good ol') Salvation Army.

Can't sleep? Watch cars in Waimea: A caller said someone was lying on the roof of Ishii's store in Waimea. Police found a young man, who said he had gone up there to watch the cars and had fallen asleep. Police reports said the cops had a very hard time awakening him and there was a strong odor of liquor about him, but the man climbed down. Police didn't arrest him because it is apparently not illegal to sleep on a roof.

Help not wanted... A report of an "unresponsive male" who had been brought in from the ocean fronting Mokihana in Waipouli turned out to be a man who had either jumped or fallen from a kayak and appeared to be floating face-down in the water. Someone had swum out and brought him to shore, but he kept trying to go back in the water. He obviously had been drinking, and he wouldn't let paramedics get near him, so they turned the case over to the police. Officers had to handcuff him to take him to the hospital for a checkup.

At the hospital, the man refused to let a doctor look at him, and he asked police if he was under arrest. When the officers said no, that they just wanted him to have a checkup, the man said he didn't want one. The officers then took off the cuffs, and he was last seen lurching around the hospital parking lot.

Taking the western or eastern route? A man called police from Honolulu saying he was worried that his mother was going to commit suicide. Officers checked and found that the mother and her husband had been drinking, she was depressed, and maybe her son had inferred she was going to kill herself because she told him on the phone that she was going to walk into the ocean and swim to Germany.

Bank Robbed for Practice
(Which all participants needed)

Back in 1979, head honchos at the Kaua'i Police Department decided that because there hadn't been a bank holdup here in - well, maybe never, the department needed some practice in foiling bank robbers. So as a training exercise, the KPD staged a robbery of American Savings & Loan in Lihu'e. And while they eventually "caught their man," some of the action read like a script from a Broadway comedy.

Major Abe Waimau and Lt. Frank Bukoski wrote the scenario, with the knowledge of Chief Roy Hiram. And AS&L manager Bob Yotsuda was in on it, and had told his employees about it, figuring it would be good training for them also.

Only the three police officers and the "robber" – a recruit, so the cops wouldn't necessarily recognize him – knew when the robbery would take place.

The plan was that a teller at the bank would activate the silent alarm that is keyed into the Honolulu Hot Line, which in turn calls the KPD to notify it of a robbery. The scriptwriters had notified the staff at the Hot Line that it was all a training exercise and not to worry, but somebody neglected to tell Yotsuda that because the Hot Line wouldn't be calling

KPD, it was his job to call the local police, direct, to report the "crime" (a fateful mistake).

So, Wednesday morning, promptly at 9:30, the "robber" entered the bank.

The teller knew that something like this might happen, but she didn't know when. So when it actually happened, she wasn't sure if this was really IT, and she just stood there, mesmerized. She said later that she was scared and she was hoping the "robber" would burst out laughing and say it was all a joke. By the time she had recovered sufficiently to press the alarm, the "robber" had fled on foot.

The officers stationed as observers across the street waited for word from the dispatcher that there had been a robbery… and they waited… and they waited.

When nothing had happened by 9:49, Chief Hiram went into the bank and discovered that Yotsuda hadn't been told that the Hot Line would ignore the alarm and that they were waiting for him to call KPD. That meant that the chief himself had to call his own dispatcher to report that a major crime had taken place.

The response time for the police – once they got the call – was excellent. It turned out that was the only excellent thing about the whole exercise. A patrolman and his sergeant arrived at the bank within one or two minutes after dispatch gave him the word.

The officer got a description of the "robber" from the teller and called dispatch, asking them to transmit an APB immediately, saying, "This is a simulated robbery, and we're looking for a local male suspect about 5' 10" tall, about 250 pounds, with a moustache, wearing jeans, a red t-shirt and, possibly, rubber slippers."

The first detective arrived a minute or two after the patrol sergeant, and within five minutes, the place was crawling with cops. Because the teller said the robber escaped on foot, police assumed that he was still on foot, so they searched high and low for him. At 10:05 a.m., only 35 minutes after the robbery, one of the officers radioed in and said he had found the suspect and was bringing him into the station for booking. A call went out for the teller, so she could come to the station to make positive identification of the suspect. But she took one look and said, "That's not the man."

The man shanghaied by the cop was instead a poor innocent bystander. He had a moustache, red t-shirt and jeans, but he was a long way from being 5' 10" and 250 pounds. At 10:16 a.m., a little more than an hour after the APB went out, officers apprehended "robber" Gary Costa. He was sitting at the Kress Store lunch counter, drinking many cups of coffee with none other than Chief Roy Hiram (who, though good-natured, must have been wondering when his recruit was going to be arrested).

Needless to say, the chief called a meeting that afternoon to critique the training exercise (while it was still fresh in everybody's minds). First of all, it was noted that while the robber had driven to the bank, just because he left on foot didn't mean he didn't have a car. Waimau and Bukoski's script had called for the robber to leave the bank, throw away a pack of matches that would have provided a clue, and leave by car. The cops failed to find the matches.

They also failed to find his car because they weren't looking for one. That pointed up another weakness – in questioning witnesses. The officers had done a good job with the one teller, but they should have questioned everyone in the bank as they were supposed to. If they had, they would have found (as per the script) that one of the other tellers could have told them that the robber had left in a car rather than on foot.

After running out of the bank, the robber had gotten into his car and driven it around the block, then parked in a no-parking zone right in front of Kress Store, across the street from the bank. The car had been there for a long time (a huge hint) with patrolmen driving by and failing to stop and ticket the car.

In addition to driving right past the illegally parked car while looking for a man on foot, not surprisingly, it didn't occur to them that the robber might have stopped off at the Kress Store lunch counter for a few cups of coffee to wait till the heat was off.

It should be noted that in the real world, there were two auto accidents with injuries at the same time, and of course, dispatch gave those assignments precedence over a mock robbery.

A point that was brought out was that excited people have a hard time giving an accurate description of a suspect – a man pointing a gun at you may look six feet tall rather than 5' 6"– and that three witnesses may give three different stories. The detective who arrested the innocent bystander knew this happens frequently, so he depended more on the moustache and clothing than on the description of the man's size, although in this case, the teller gave a pretty accurate description.

The police found that although their response time was good – crucial in such a crime – their biggest problem was that nobody knew who was in charge. They realized that they had to rewrite their procedures and make sure they're understood. And sometimes who's in charge sounds like Abbott and Costello's "Who's on First?" routine: It's the patrol sergeant who's in charge first, but if a patrol lieutenant arrives, then he's in charge, but only until a detective shows up because then, even though the detective is at a sergeant's level, he outranks the lieutenant because of the type of crime. But for a different type of crime…

Despite the problems, Waimau and Deputy Chief Ray Duvauchelle agreed that the exercise had been good training, and because it wasn't real, some of it was – in true Kaua'i tradition – good fun.

P.S.… Kaua'i has since had a few bank robberies. The first one was the best. In the early 1980s, a man 6 feet 5 inches tall and barefoot, took a cab to First Hawaiian Bank in Lihu'e, asked the driver to wait, and entered the bank with a paper sack and a toy gun, and demanded cash. He came out a few minutes later, got into the cab, and told the driver to take him to the airport.

Police apprehended him a short time later, having the advantage of information from numerous bystanders on Rice Street, who would certainly notice probably the tallest man on the island at that time. While taxis were not unheard of then, they were certainly uncommon idling outside banks. Police took the poor soul to Mahelona Hospital so he could tell a doctor about his troubles and aspirations.

In the second robbery, of the Bank of Hawai'i's Kapa'a branch, the man wore a disguise (something necessary here), and it took detectives several days to track him to his home in Hanama'ulu.

The third robbery was of a savings and loan office in Kapa'a, and police captured their man just 20 minutes later.

Significantly (and maybe unfortunately for their getaway chances), none of the robbers stopped by the Kress Store lunch counter to have a cup of coffee with the chief of police.

"Take your time, Miss, we want to be sure. Hats off again please."

High Times & Misdemeanors

Drinking was a big part of the social life on this island until recent years. You went to a local bar to forget your troubles, not to talk about them. There were usually a lot of laughs and you frequently drank with the intention of getting drunk.

Often the amount of alcohol consumed was amazing. Local drinkers could pass out slowly. If a doctor from the mainland saw them, he'd swear they were unconscious, but all of a sudden, they'd sit up and go back to strumming their guitars or 'ukuleles without missing a beat.

Being drunk wasn't shameful and drunks weren't shunned. I remember after one graduation lu'au, the kids piled a very inebriated Uncle George into the car and they all raced off to go dancing at Club Jetty.

There weren't many cars on the road, so there were fewer accidents than one might imagine. You knew if a policeman stopped you for weaving on the highway, you would not only know him or be related to him, he'd drive you home if you were really in bad shape. If you could still manage, he would follow you to make sure you got home safely.

The great increase in the number of cars on the island's

single highway, the corresponding rise in both the number and severity of accidents, the strict enforcement of drunk driving laws, and the terrible penalties imposed by the insurance companies have altered the social life of many, many people here. No more devoting Sundays to drinking in the local bars. Luʻaus and garage parties that used to last until 4 a.m. are now pau before midnight. There is also less absenteeism on Mondays, which were referred to as "Hawaiian holidays."

It's not easy being easy... A Michigan man who had been staying on a boat in Nawiliwili Harbor had a very bad night. He borrowed a friend's car – without permission – had too much to drink and drove into the ocean. When he managed to get out of the car and back to shore, police were standing there waiting to arrest him on charges of drunk driving and auto theft.

Well, you said stop: Responding to a report that a pedestrian had been struck by a truck in Poʻipu, police couldn't find any sign of a struck pedestrian. They learned later that a beer-impaired passenger standing in the bed of the pickup truck had pounded on the cab of the truck for the driver to stop. The driver did. The passenger didn't. He went sailing over the cab and landed on the pavement. His friends took him to the hospital, where doctors treated him for a broken collar bone and a lot of road rash.

Early harvest: A man failed to negotiate a turn on the road to Kokeʻe, and his car careened into a cane field and burst into flames. He was able to crawl out in time to avoid the fire, but also in time to get a ticket for drunk driving and maybe to pay for the $59,000 in cane he "harvested before its time."

"There's my boat!"

Boat on the road, driver still at sea... A Waimea man was towing his boat on Kaumuali'i Highway just west of Kaumakani at about 2 a.m. when he looked in the rearview mirror and noticed that the boat was no longer behind him.

He turned around and drove back, looking for his boat. He'd driven about a mile when he saw it sitting on the highway. A KPD officer was directing traffic around it. The man disregarded the officer's directions and instead plowed headlong into his boat, knocking it off the trailer (which created even more of a mess).

The police charged him with drunk driving and reckless endangering (and his boat was probably never quite the same).

Disagreement resolved... Police received a report of an assault at Kalapaki Beach over who stole whose pot plants, but by the time police arrived, both participants were completely "mellowed out."

Stir crazy: With two Australian and one U.S. Navy ship docked at Nawiliwili, and hundreds of sailors on shore leave for the weekend, KPD beefed up its patrols and maintained peace, relatively speaking. The sailors kept cash registers ringing in bars from Lihu'e to Kapa'a, but only about a dozen passed out and had to be taken back to their ships by friends or the shore patrol.

The one exception: A sailor whose good judgment deserted him stole a car parked near the docks. He zoomed off, but had gone only a short distance when he ran smack into a coconut tree. The car was destroyed but the sailor was apparently relaxed enough to have escaped injury. Police initially charged him with auto theft, but dropped the charge when he managed to scrape together the $200 that satisfied the owner as to the value of the car, even before it hit the tree.

Opium reported... Vice officers went to investigate a report of opium growing on the West side. They used a 4-wheel-drive to get up into the mountains, where they discovered a rare Hawaiian poppy. While that may warm the hearts of botanists, it isn't an opiate.

The magic mushroom juice defense: On trial for burglary, disorderly conduct, terroristic threatening, and indecent exposure, a man offered this defense:

He said he was living at Anini Beach Park, and one day

decided to go jogging. He became thirsty, so he asked a "hippie-looking guy" for a drink of his tea. He had guzzled most of the drink when the hippie-looking guy laughed and told him the "tea" contained "mushroom juice."

Whatever was in the tea, the defendant claimed, is what prompted him to break into the home of a Kilauea woman he didn't know, run in and out and trash the place. It was the tea, he claimed, that caused him to start screaming, "I'm God, kill the Fat Man!" And it was the tea that made him climb up onto a rock wall and drop his pants.

However, the prosecutor pointed out, even the defendant's own witness testified that he had seen the man merely take a sip of the tea and immediately spit it out. She also noted that the defendant had told a doctor during his post-arrest psychiatric evaluation that he'd eaten magic mushrooms he'd picked in a nearby pasture, and that lab tests indicated there were amphetamines in his blood.

The jury didn't buy the defendant's defense. It found him guilty of one felony and three misdemeanors.

Picture this... A vice officer followed an informant to a large marijuana patch, and midway through the field, the officer decided to return to his car and get his camera. When he got back to the patch, he was crawling around on his hands and knees looking for the informant - when he and the suspect grower, who was also crawling around on all fours, banged heads.

The unexpected encounter startled them both, and the cop wasn't even sure he had managed to get a picture before the grower took off, on two feet. But the cop did harvest the pakalolo plants, 3-7 ft. tall, and weighing over 100 pounds.

"You have the right to remain silent..."

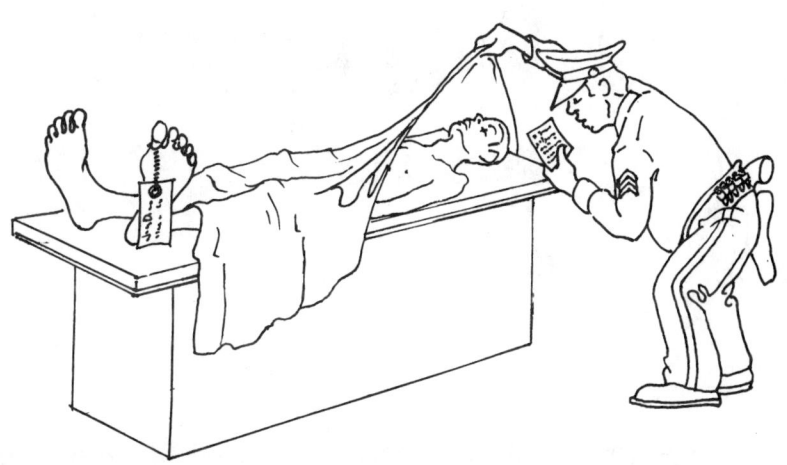

Cop's motto — never say die: A man in his late 20s was involved in a bad accident near Koloa. Paramedics brought him to Wilcox Hospital, but he died and, being obviously if unofficially dead, was taken to the morgue. There police found $5,000 in cash and some cocaine in his pocket, and that was added to the coke, heroin and pot police had found in his car. So while the man was laid out on the slab, vice officer Pat Layosa read him his rights, then arrested him on a felony drug charge — just before the doctor arrived and pronounced the guy officially dead (Pat was always one for covering all the bases).

This is not thinking ahead: A prisoner at the old "Wailua Hilton" jail, coming back to his cell after his day on work release, first went around to the back of the building and tossed a bag of marijuana through the bars of his cell, then went around to the front to be let in. He was admitted by the jailer, who was waiting for him, pakalolo in hand.

Puhi pakalolo:
here, there, everywhere

Back in 1979, police went to raid a Puhi house that an informant told them had marijuana plants growing in the yard. They went to the wrong house. Not to worry. By the end of the day, the cops had, by accident, discovered and confiscated 143 plants weighing 237 pounds from eight patches at seven houses – all in Puhi.

Detectives Frank Silva and Pat Ornellas first went to the house in the Old Puhi plantation camp that they thought the anonymous informant had described. We'll call it House #1. It was the wrong house. While at the wrong house, they happened to look over into the yard of the house next door (House #2), and what did they see? Pot plants. They pulled them up. Then they went off to find the *right* House #1.

They did, and they found the plants as the informant had described. Rather than pulling the plants immediately, Silva and Ornellas decided to get a search warrant so they could make an arrest. But then, as fate would have it, they changed their minds and decided instead to go see the owner of the house at his job in Koloa to make sure the plants were really his. (Detective Pat Layosa explained this consideration stems from the fact that older people often don't even know what marijuana looks like, and so sometimes kids take advantage of that and plant the illegal weeds in less-suspect yards.)

So, as Silva and Ornellas drove off to Koloa, a woman who recognized them – probably from gambling raids – started going from house to house, alerting the neighbors by yelling, "Vice officers! Vice officers!"

Next came a call to KPD – a Puhi woman reporting that there was a burglar in her yard. Officer William Ka'auwai responded. At the woman's house (yep, House #3), he saw marijuana leaves on the ground. He asked her if vice officers had been there and she said she didn't know. When she took Ka'auwai to her backyard, reachable only by going through a goat pen, he discovered marijuana plants growing there and he called for assistance from a vice officer.

Still looking for a burglar, Ka'auwai went to a nearby house, where one could get to the backyard only through an elderly man's bedroom. The man gave Ka'auwai permission to pass, and the officer found marijuana plants in this backyard also. House #4.

Meanwhile, Layosa, Lt. Frank Bukoski, and patrolmen Larry Fernandes, John Ka'auwai and Milton Ching, all in the area, responded to the burglary and marijuana calls.

Layosa, first to arrive, heard Ornellas radioing in to go to House #1 (by which they meant the *right* House #1). But Layosa, like Ornellas before him, also turned into the wrong driveway, but a *different* wrong driveway (House #5), saw a patch of marijuana and confiscated it.

Ornellas and Silva, returning from Koloa, went back to the right House #1, and, having decided the owner knew nothing about the plants, pulled them up. Meanwhile, as Layosa and Ka'auwai were tying House #5's plants onto their car, some kids appeared on the scene, saw them, and took off running. The cops pursued them, and enroute, stumbled over another patch of pakalolo – at House #6.

Soon after, Ornellas happened onto one more patch – at House #7.

After two hours, the officers finally found each other and tried to figure out just what had happened. As the pieces began to fit together, they realized they had actually hit eight different patches (at seven houses), mostly because so many of them went to the wrong houses to start with.

The next day, elsewhere, and with much less confusion, vice officers picked up 21 pounds of marijuana from three patches, one in Koloa and two in Kalaheo. In one of the yards, someone had intertwined white rose vines with the pakalolo plants, but the officers recognized the weed anyway and also confiscated the white roses.

Overheard on the Scanner

The scanner was a source not only of crucial information but of both intentional and unintentional humor. It should be noted that gambling is illegal on Kaua'i. Also, that is a pretty well accepted part of life here.

A new communications system has helped the police immeasurably, but it's also made the scanner a lot less valuable and fun for me.

The dispatcher said a caller complained that the participants in a local gambling game were getting too loud. The beat officer checked and said, "Forty to fifty players in the Koloa game, but they'll quiet down because I told them if they don't, I'll call the vice guys."

An officer goes into a house on River Street, next to the canal in Kapa'a - gambling central on the Garden Island - to ask one of the women to call her son on the west side. He walks into the gambling game. He leaves, play resumes, he calls in, "Message delivered."

Looking for a runaway: The dispatcher said, "As per the mother, she said her daughter is 4 feet, 11 inches, long dark hair and a long-sleeved sweat shirt. Oh yeah, she said she acts like one *tita!*"

In a radio exchange between patrol officers about a man with a rifle roaming around, perhaps intending to hit a gambling game: "Call Eclipse's place and see if they get any games tonight."
"What about that other, *da kine*, place?"
"Nah, they only get games on Sunday."

"The guy in the wheelchair is drunk and won't set up his tent." (???)

The paramedic: "An 85-year-old woman came to the front desk and said she fell. She's inebriated and hard of hearing so we can't get a past medical history on her, but blood pressure is 108/83. Man, she's lookin' good!"

"The girl left Mahelona [psychiatric hospital] without permission. She's five-two, dark hair, Filipino… and oh yeah, she's wearing a blanket."

"The jailer called and said there's a drunk outside pounding on the door wanting to get in."

Dispatcher: "His wife called and said her [drunken] husband wants his car, so you've got a problem." Patrol Sgt. Ronnie Holt says, "No, I've got his keys, so *he's* got a problem."

Beat officer calling in after responding to a report of a problem: "Everything cool! Conk on the head. One time 'nuff."

Dispatcher: "Headquarters to all units. What is the weather like in your area? The Weather Bureau is inquiring."

Cops 'n' Robbers

In the 1980s, Kauaʻi police arrested three of their Honolulu colleagues for the armed robbery of participants in a gambling game on River Street in Kapaʻa. Coming from a big city, the Honolulu cops apparently didn't realize just how small Kauaʻi is.

The trio wore ski masks and carried guns when they staged the robbery. Police were called as soon as the men left, and although no one had seen the faces of the robbers, it was reported that they sped off in a gold-colored rental car. Police immediately threw up a roadblock at the Wailua Bridge because there's no way to get from Kapaʻa to Lihuʻe Airport without crossing the bridge. But they waited, and they waited, and no gold-colored car drove by.

As it turned out, the three men hadn't headed for the airport, but instead had driven to the home of an uncle of one of the trio, in Wailua Homesteads, and asked if they could stay for the night. In true aloha style, they were welcomed. That night, the three men went into Kapaʻa town to have a few drinks at the Oceanview Bar. They left the island the following day.

But little did they know that this island is so small that:

* their car was the only gold-colored rental car on the island at that time;

* three burly strangers in a local bar is unusual and was noticed;

* at least one of the gamblers who had been robbed that day by three burly strangers was drinking in the Oceanview that very night, and although he hadn't seen their faces, he felt the coincidence was suspicious and told police.

Another thing they didn't realize about this small island: The uncle they were staying with was also a police commissioner. When the uncle heard about the robbery the next day, he began wondering about the suitcase his nephew left at his house. Finally he looked inside and found ski masks and guns, and being a good citizen as well as a commissioner, he reported it to the police.

The trio also didn't realize that the off-duty officer at the airport, who knew one of the guys from school days and greeted them warmly, would put two and two together and reported his conclusion.

So when it became obvious that KPD's detectives were going to have to go to Oʻahu to arrest three fellow police officers, the tension around the station that day was palpable and contagious. By the time the arrests were made and the HPD officers were brought into the Lihuʻe station for booking late that night, I was so nervous, my hands were shaking and I wasn't sure I could operate my camera. I did get a couple of usable shots, however.

And the following morning I wrote one of my favorite lead paragraphs… "Last night, nine police officers boarded the plane for the last flight to Kauaʻi. Six of them were carrying guns and three of them wore handcuffs."

The three officers were fired from the Honolulu Police Department because they had already acquired dubious reputations. But they had the money to hire a good attorney and he (wisely) kept getting continuances from the court. The case dragged on for several years, and the memories of the gamblers got weaker and weaker. Not only had they not seen the faces of the robbers, but because the game was illegal to start with, they weren't eager to get up on the stand and testify.

It was also never established how much money the robbers got because gamblers don't like to talk (especially in court) about how much they take into a game or out of it. The state's case fizzled and eventually the trio got a deferred acceptance of their guilty (DAG) pleas to greatly reduced charges.

A P.S. to that story... The need for money and the willingness to go to any lengths to get it continued with at least one member of that infamous trio. More than 20 years later, one of the former HPD officers who managed to get his criminal record expunged (when the DAG plea period was pau), and to land himself a cushy job with the state where he'd gotten promoted to captain in the crash fire unit at the airport on the little island of Lanaʻi, was arrested again.

Thomas Decano, Jr., was carrying $50,000 in cash when he was apprehended as he got off a plane in Honolulu. He was charged with stealing it from the mail at the airport on the Pineapple Island, and he admitted that gambling was (one of) his problems. The former police officer/fireman is now serving a two-year prison term.

POLICE BLOTTER 111

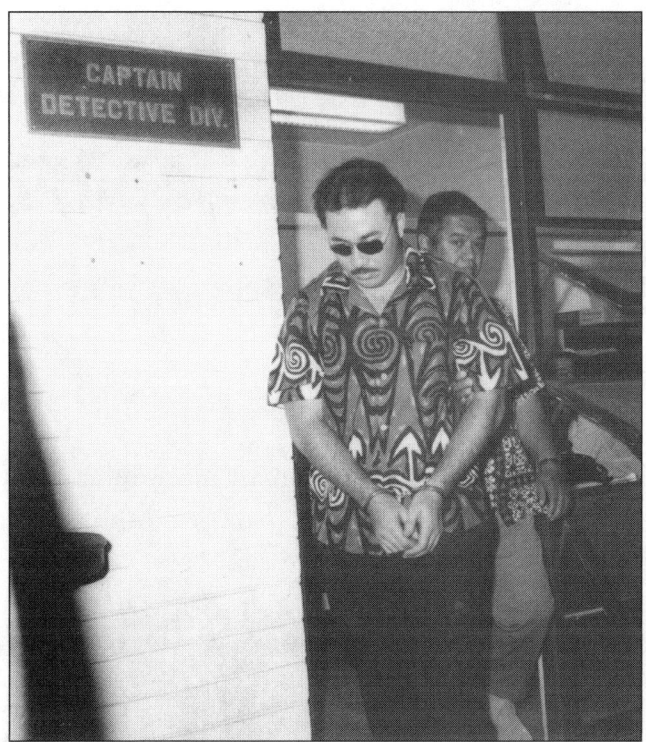

HONOLULU COP Thomas Decano, Jr., at KPD headquarters in 1975 after his arrest with two fellow officers, for robbery of a gambling game on Kaua'i, with KPD's detective Sam Sheldon right behind him. Decano was arrested again, for theft, 20 years later. (photo by Georgia Mossman's shaking hands)

Miscellaneous Kine Reports

All kinds of friendship... One man hit another man on the head with a baseball bat, but the batee said the batter was his friend (?) so he didn't want to press charges... an officer served a warrant, an order to appear in court, with a female name and an AKA (also known as) a male name, and it turned out it was someone who hasn't been able to afford a sex change operation yet... and a Nawiliwili man said he bought something from a friend, but after he was arrested for possession of stolen property, he's re-evaluating the "friendship."

Gate-crashing is a federal offense: A Kaua'i man who drove his pickup truck through the closed gate of the Kilauea Point National Wildlife Refuge paid dearly for the federal crime. The federal district court sentenced the Kilauea resident to six months in prison and ordered him to pay almost $3,000 as restitution for the cost of repairs. The U.S. Fish and Wildlife Service owns the refuge, which provides habitat for the endangered nene (Hawaiian goose), shearwaters and other sea birds. The gate was part of a fence designed to keep out predators such as dogs and cats.

Unusual happenings can be reasonable... there was a request for police to investigate some helicopter landings atop Sleeping Giant Mountain in Wailua, where landings are not ordinarily allowed. It turned out that pilot Jack Harter was providing transportation for officials doing a geological survey.

Smoker not carted off airplane in chains: A woman either so hooked on cigarettes or so afraid of flying that she couldn't last the 30 minutes it took to get from Honolulu to Lihu'e without a puff, was sniffed out in an Aloha Airlines jet by a passenger and a flight attendant.

The woman had entered the lavatory, disarmed the smoke alarm by rermoving the battery, inhaled on her cigarette, discarded the butt, and returned to her seat. A passenger sitting near the lavatory smelled smoke and alerted the flight attendant. The attendant tracked the smell down and discovered the disarmed alarm. Apparently possessed of a bloodhound-quality olfactory organ, she then went snuffling down the aisle, stopping at the seat of the woman, whom the passenger then identified as having just come out of the lavatory.

The culprit smoker first denied disarming the smoke detector, but when the plane landed in Lihu'e and airport security accosted her, she spilled the beans and turned over the pilfered battery. Officials also "tossed" the lavatory and came up with the telltale cigarette butt.

But despite the threat of dire consequences of the in-flight warning, the woman wasn't placed in chains and carted off to San Quentin. Instead, airport officials turned the case over to the Federal Aviation Administration.

At press time, the woman was facing up to a $1,000 civil fine. If she decided to be "difficult" about it, there was a chance she'd have to face the U.S. Attorney in Honolulu.

Just Wanted Some Attention: At 2 a.m. in Hanalei Bay, a 38-year-old Honolulu man pulled up anchor on his boat with two young, reluctant shipmates from Oʻahu aboard and set sail. The older man appeared intent on committing suicide and took out a gun, saying he was going to shoot himself. One of the younger men wrested the gun from him and removed the bullets. The man got the gun back, put it to his head and pulled the trigger, but it didn't go off. Then, however, he fell overboard.

After his companions retrieved him from the sea, he told them "you won't see me again," and promptly jumped back into the ocean. The companions threw out flotation gear and although they had no lights, they said they searched the area for about 45 minutes before they headed back to shore to report the man missing at sea.

Police, the Coast Guard and next of kin were notified and a search began. It was called off when it was learned that the missing man apparently hadn't been as serious about killing himself as it seemed, for he had swum three miles to shore and climbed back aboard his boat at 8 a.m.

The truck, the doghouse and the little boy: A Kauaʻi man was helping a family move from Puhi to Lihuʻe. He put the family's large doghouse in the bed of his pickup truck, and he let the parents' six-year-old boy ride inside the doghouse.

The man didn't tie the doghouse down, and it flew off the truck near Puhi. The boy suffered a broken leg. Police cited the driver for driving without a license and for allowing a child to ride in the bed of a truck. The insurance company of the driver's mother, who owned the truck, settled the case for more than $100,000.

POLICE BLOTTER 115

Overwhelming Force: Eight plainclothes officers on a special weekend detail in Nawiliwili responded to a report of one man acting up in a nightclub. The club owner, not realizing that the eight were cops, called police and said there were nine people having a fight. Officers back at the station, hearing there was a big fight, raced to the scene, so that the nightclub was swarming with policemen – far outnumbering the nightclub patrons – over what was a misunderstanding about a minor incident.

He just couldn't resist... A male from the audience at the Roxy Theater in Kapaʻa went up on stage to pat one of the pretty oil wrestlers on the *okole*, which led to his being charged with assault (with a friendly weapon?)... someone not passing with care knocked down a "Pass With Care" sign . . . a police officer drove over a woman's golf clubs, so the county agreed to buy her a new set of clubs... and a Princeville man faces a charge of false reporting to law enforcement officials for allegedly giving them some *"wrong misinformation"* about who was the driver and who was the passenger in a recent traffic accident.

Assault of a sexual nature... a report that a Wailua woman had been sexually assaulted turned out to be a case of her ear being abused with lurid suggestions over the phone by some jerk who thought he was a smooth talker... a report of cruelty to animals in Kapahi (maybe chickens with spurs?)... and a request for police to make a stroll-through at a Kapaʻa bar where trouble was brewing.

A lazy, dazey afternoon... there was a report that an employee at a big discount store had brought some "special kine" homemade brownies to work, which were seized and turned over to police (because while that pakalolo may make for a more pleasant afternoon, it's illegal).

"Aloha Grandpa, aloha..."

What better way to go? A nine-year-old boy sitting up in a tree watched his 69-year-old grandpa throw net, saw him sit down on the reef and not move; he had died doing what he loved most.

All kinds of neighbors... A caller said her neighbor had taken off his clothes and was displaying his "wares" in his picture window... the Blotter said Melody Stevenson of Anahola found a "spectacle" on the side of the road (and while that's certainly a possibility, we feel pretty sure that what she found was a pair of eyeglasses)... and some jerk damaged a police blue-&-white in Club Jetty's parking lot, while the officer was "off his car," responding to a call for help.

The Naked Blotter

For some reason – maybe it's the warm climate, maybe it's that tropical feeling that anything goes – people on Kaua'i get naked, or find themselves somehow naked, more than in most places. For example:

There was a report that a young woman came out of her house dressed only in her birthday suit. Not surprisingly, a nearby yard man stared at her, and she came over and punched him. He went to Wilcox Hospital, more for protection against being called a rapist than for the seriousness of the injuries.

A caller said there was a woman in distress and waving for help about 1,500 yards offshore in Wailua. Firemen flew out in the Air One rescue chopper, but the woman, who was backstroking along in the buff (she's a powerful long-distance swimmer well known – by now – to police), told them that she didn't need any help and backstroked away.

A report from a South Shore tour company that a passenger aboard their boat had taken off all his clothes and refused to put them back on. The trip was canceled, everyone was returned to shore, and the incident was listed as sexual assault 5th degree.

Called to Kojima's Laundromat on a report of "man in dryer," police helped him out of the dryer; then they were called back when the same man was sitting there in the nude waiting for his clothes to dry… there was a report of a West side man wearing only a mask over his face… and police found a nude man sleeping in his car in Kapaia who said he thought he had lost his clothes the night before, but he couldn't remember just how or where.

There was a report of a man walking around the Coconut Marketplace "bottomless," but police couldn't find anyone fitting that description…there were reports of a woman without any clothes on riding a swing in Wiliko Park, a nude man in the bushes in ʻAliomanu, a naked man at Waimea Landing, a woman running around without any clothes on at Banyan Harbor condos, an inebriated woman running around nude in a Kapaʻa restaurant, two males without bathing suits, causing quite a ripple at the Waiʻohai Hotel's Terrace pool… and a caller said a nude man had entered his home and was causing a disturbance, but then he called back to withdraw his complaint (?).

A beachgoer reported a couple and their three children being photographed in the nude by two photographers – one nude and one clothed. He said he watched four rolls of film being shot and said the poses themselves weren't pornographic, but he was concerned about the children's welfare. An officer talked to the mother, and she said she knew the photographers. The pictures were for *Naturalist* magazine, which is popular in Europe, and she said she got paid enough to be able to buy food for the kids.

Someone was disturbed enough about a topless sunbather near the Holiday Inn that he/she/it called police, and the officer, taught to be no judge of beauty in cases like this, listed the incident as indecent exposure... and responding to a call, police found a naked man walking along the road in Po'ipu Beach; he put his clothes back on at their request and told the officers that he was just trying to get rid of his girlfriend.(?)

Police found a naked man in the restroom at the airport. He said he had torn up his clothes and was cleansing himself in preparation for a meeting with God. Security officers scouted up some clothing, and police took him to Mahelona so he could discuss his situation with a psychiatrist there.

Another naked man was harassing visitors at the Hanalei Valley lookout, and police arrested him for open lewdness when they found him strolling along Kuhio Highway, still naked... a woman at Lihu'e Laundromat told police a man completely undressed in front of her, apparently wanting to wash *all* his clothes... and a male was "streaking" through Kiahuna Village Shopping Center in Po'ipu, wearing only a t-shirt, and that was pulled up over his face.

Security at The Market Place in Wailua called police to remove a drunk from the shopping center. The officer decided that the man was more disturbed than drunk, so he took the guy to Mahelona Hospital, where the staffer said there was no doctor on duty, so could he please come back tomorrow?

A while later, police got a report of the same guy running around nude at the airport. They arrested him and charged him with a misdemeanor, and he posted bail. Still later, police got another report of an auto accident on the West side, with the driver - the same guy - fleeing from the scene. Naked.

Piliwaiwai
(GAMBLING) ON KAUA'I: A WAY OF LIFE

Gambling has always been illegal on Kaua'i and it has always been a big part of life here. The chicken fights are held from early spring until the fall, when the chickens molt; then it's betting on the football games; and there are card and dice games held almost every day, year round.

The chicken fights...

Chicken fights are a Filipino import, and aficionados often claim it is a "cultural tradition" as much as football is a great American sport. While "the chickens" are dominated by Filipinos, Kauaians of all ethnic groups attend and bet on the outcome of the fights. And each town or area has its own gaff specialist, the person they believe can make the best or the sharpest razor to attach to the chicken's leg, and now, they may even import gaffs from the mainland.

Back when most of the big fights and derbys were held mainly at three arenas – in Kapahi, Koloa and Kekaha – there were also card and dice games and food booths, which made the events more like a social gathering than a furtive pastime.

The games were never wide open, but everyone knew pretty much when and where they were, including the police.

Occasionally pressure would build for some law enforcement action, but one of the biggest problems was finding someone to infiltrate the games who wouldn't be recognized. Some of the police efforts over the years have looked more like comedy routines than raids.

One officer said he was enlisted to go undercover when he was a recruit, and when he got there, he discovered his father-in-law was among the bettors. He had attempted a disguise, but he was so nervous, fearing he'd be recognized and expecting someone to yell *"COPS!"* at any time, that he could hardly pay attention to what was going on, let alone come up with credible evidence.

There's big money to be made in the chicken fights, however, and every so often gamblers from other islands come over and try to horn in on the action. The police do step in then and try for arrests if possible, and settle for harassment if necessary. They probably will never be able to shut the fights down completely, so their goal seems to be to "keep it down and keep it local."

Over the years, raids have occasionally led to some lifetime gamblers being charged with cruelty to animals and paying *manini* (small) fines. The few times there have been felony gambling charges, the gamblers have been sentenced on charges reduced to misdemeanors.

Police try to prevent war: In the late 1970s, in an all-out effort to cut down on gambling and to avoid a "war" over the operations here, Kaua'i police raided and broke up gambling games at three different locations over one weekend.

At noon Saturday, armed with 15 men and a search warrant, Lt. Howard Carvalho raided the Eclipse's home in Kekaha. The cops blocked the two exits and secured the area so none of the more than 90 people present could leave. Police then confiscated a dice table, a crap table bumper, dice, dice cups, and a scale used to weigh chickens. They searched everyone and confiscated a number of gaffs and knives. They then photographed everyone in groups of five.

Sunday at 9:30 a.m., KPD's vice unit raided the old Kealia Camp, where about 200 people had gathered. They had set up two food booths, and were getting the chickens ready to fight and the cards shuffled so the monte game could begin. Police broke up the game and suggested everyone just go home peacefully and watch the basketball game on TV.

Carvalho said apparently he wasn't very persuasive, because when they raided old Jack Lai's Camp near Anahola at 1:30 p.m., about 100 - of the same people who had been at Kealia Camp, and the food booths, had just changed locations. By that time, police were able to discourage them from moving on to still another location that day.

Lt. Carvalho reports that Floro Villabrille, who ran the biggest fights on the island, followed the court injunction against gambling at his arena in Keapana. The gates remained padlocked and there was no action there over the weekend.

(When Villabrille decided to get out of the chicken-fighting business, he wisely decided that the way to end the use of his arena, and to prevent a takeover, was to subdivide the land. I have never seen government officials grant subdivision approval so quickly.

(It should be noted also that aside from being the "main man" in chicken fighting on the island, Floro was an otherwise good citizen and a generous man. He also held the world crown in escrima, a martial arts form using sticks that is popular in the Philippines, and he gave instructions in the art to several Kaua'i police officers.)

Forfeiture law forces changes. What has seemed to make more of an impression on the gamblers than anything else is the asset forfeiture law. Nothing big has been seized yet, but the threat of losing one's home or property by holding chicken fights and card games has made for some interesting "floating" fights, in pastures and even cemeteries. It's not really known if that has reduced the number of gamblers, but it definitely seems to have made the players much more close-mouthed about the fights.

Then there's sports betting... While the Filipinos may favor "the chickens," it's the Japanese who are most commonly involved in sports betting. By October, when the chicken fights have come to a halt, football betting gets into full swing. And for many Kauaians, football isn't football without betting.

In October 1995, Kaua'i police busted runners for a 6-5 gambling ring. The men were then released pending further investigation and possible indictment by the grand jury. (The betting sheets included the names of many government officials and not surprisingly, the case never made it to the grand jury.)

Sgt. Wilfred Ihu explained that in 6-5, the runners distribute the betting sheets for the house. The bettor weighs the odds and point spreads – often after $15- to $30-phone calls to advertised national "experts" for advice – and marks his bets. The runner then picks up the sheet and takes it to one of the three or four houses on the island.

There's no up-front money involved. Winners get $5 per game. Losers pay $6, plus 20 percent "juice" for the house. The $5-bet is only in principle, however, because most houses don't accept bets for less than $25.

In the fall, on Saturday, there can be as many as 35 college football games to bet on; then there are the Sunday pro games, and the Monday night pro games, when those who lost big bucks over the weekend "chase"– making even bigger bets to try to recover their losses. Then there are the holiday bowl games, when betting skyrockets as gamblers continue their chase.

"But the only real winner is the house, because it has and keeps the odds in its favor," Ihu said.

(To give you an idea of how big sports gambling is on this little island, which was economically depressed at the time, there was about $500,000 in bets placed at three or four "houses" in a three-day period between Christmas and New Year's. So you can guess how big it must be statewide. But like the gambling itself, you never hear any conversation about games, bets, winners or losers - in public or at work - and considering the number of people who are making and losing big money, that's amazing!)

Generally, the rule for those who can't pay their gambling debts is "no pay, no play," but even on friendly, casual Kaua'i, if the debts get really big, enforcers sometimes handle the collections, Ihu said.

"Gambling has gone on here for so long that it's a way of life for many people. There are senior citizens who gamble almost every day as a way of socializing, but we try to monitor things because there are also gamblers with criminal records, and now, different than in the past, some of the young guys involved are into drugs and guns," he said.

The sergeant estimated that about 5 percent of those who bet regularly are compulsive gamblers. Betting on one game after another – of whatever kind – often becomes another chase, as the eternally hopeful addict remembers his few wins and forgets his many losses. "But the odds on recovering losses are so remote that it's almost like pouring more money down a hole," he said.

Percentage-wise, Kaua'i, and Hawai'i as a whole, probably have more people who go to Las Vegas to gamble – four to five times a year regularly – than almost any other state. People usually take enough money to be able to lose at least $100 a day, and win or lose, everyone seems to have a great time betting on the tables and the slots. They see all their friends at the Hotels California and Fremont, which cater to Hawaiian visitors (serving sticky rice), and they figure that with food and lodgings so cheap, they'd spend at least that amount each day anywhere else on a vacation and not even have a chance to win that elusive million-dollar jackpot.

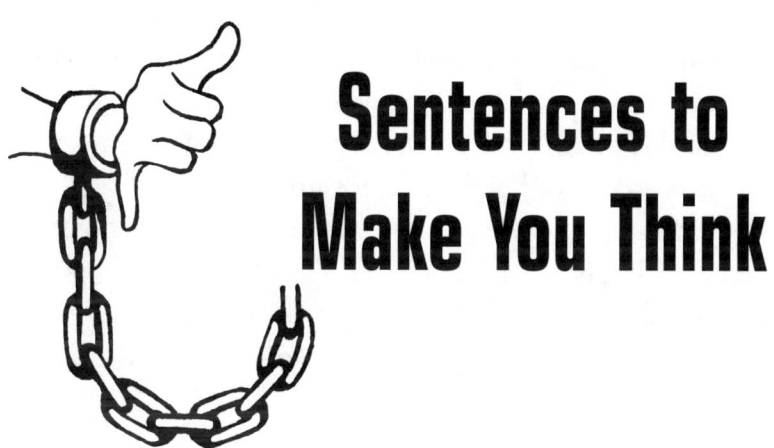

Sentences to Make You Think

It's impossible for anyone to sit through 20 years of criminal court cases, watching the trials and seeing the judge sentencing those convicted, without making some observations and forming some opinions about the criminals, the penalties, and the court procedure itself. For what it's worth, I offer some of these reflections.

When the judge passes sentences... Depending on one's experiences and expectations in life, the reactions to receiving a jail sentence vary. Some people are angry, some are resentful, some accepting. And some people are just plain petrified. I've seen defendants, facing the judge with their backs to me, so scared that I can see the cheeks of their *okoles* shaking.

Once I saw a woman just quietly slide to the floor when the the word "jail" was mentioned. The judge paused for a minute while the woman's attorney helped her back up to her feet, then the sentencing continued.

Another time, after being cuffed in preparation for being led off to jail, a young man kept saying quietly, "I can't do it. I can't do it."

It's not a question of innocence... I always wince when I see or hear reports of a defendant being found "innocent." I know the media does that to avoid the risk of leaving off the "not" when the verdict is not guilty, but it's not accurate.

Determining innocence is not what a jury does. Who could possibly judge anyone's innocence? The job of the jury is to decide, based on the evidence presented by the state, if the defendant is guilty or not guilty. If the state has met its burden of proof, he's guilty. If it hasn't, he's not guilty.

Where did it begin?... One day in district court there was an unusually large number of unusually disheveled and derelict-looking defendants, lined-up in their orange "pumpkin suits," with handcuffs and leg irons. I thought, I'm sure that almost all of these people were at one time someone's precious baby.

Remorse is required... "I'm sorry. I'll never do it again." Over and over again, that's what so many guilty defendants tell the judges. You wonder if they're truly contrite, sorry they got caught or aware that that is what they're expected to say.

Then you wonder how they have the nerve to say it when they appear before the judge again, for the same type of crime. And no doubt some of them are truly sorry each time.

What do criminals look like?... There are men and women who wear white shirts and ties (or the equivalent aloha wear) and smile as they steal thousands or even millions of dollars over a long period of time while in a position of trust. If they're convicted, they usually get a five-year prison term, then serve only 18 months because they're "not the criminal type." Two cases in particular come to mind.

One involved a woman who embezzled thousands of dollars

from a company while on probation for having done the same thing at a previous job. Both of those small businesses have now gone bankrupt, and while she's not solely responsible, she played a major role. How many small businesses can recover from the theft of $20,000 or $40,000? Yet I don't think her jail time totaled more than a year.

Then there's the one that left the whole community angry. The former county treasurer stole $1.3 million, over a period of several years, all from cash payments made by taxpayers. He was given a 10-year sentence and there was an order for restitution. He served about two years of "soft time," then was furloughed. There has never been an indication that he felt an obligation to pay one cent of restitution.

Yet, I often see kids who have stolen cars, committed some burglaries or are caught using drugs receive, and serve serious jail time.

I know the jails are overcrowded, and from the warden's point of view, when he has a nice, intelligent prisoner who doesn't cause any trouble, he wants to get rid of him to make room for someone who's "dangerous." But the rationale escapes me.

These white-collar thefts are still major crimes, even if the perpetrator is well-behaved. We're not talking rehabilitation, and "nice, respectable" criminals should serve hard time, too.

Guilty makes it absolute... To the authorities in the criminal justice system, a "guilty" verdict is accepted as absolute. The defendant is expected to be regretful from that moment on. There's simply no room in the system for anyone who denies his guilt.

The probation officer, who interviews the defendant for the preparation of a recommendation for sentencing for the judge, gives him or her very bad marks for "lack of remorse."

No doubt there are some who actually are guilty but still hold out hope for a reversal of the verdict, and some who are in denial. But those who are really not guilty (and no doubt they're few and far between) have to figure out how to live within the system that doesn't believe them.

An awful time... I'll never get used to the pity I feel when the judge says, "mitimus to issue forthwith," and the defendant, who had been sitting near me in civilian clothes, is patted down, then I hear the "click, click" of the leg irons and the cuffs, and the sobbing or quiet weeping of the family behind me.

Only the unknown deserve to die... Because Hawai'i does not have capital punishment, we're spared the decision of who must be sentenced to death. But the debate over the death penalty is ongoing here, and I've concluded that when it gets down to naming the actual people who deserve to die, the only ones who would qualify are those you don't know or don't know much about.

Maybe I've seen too many gangster movies, but rarely does anyone look evil. Even murderers have some redeeming qualities. I've yet to see anyone who didn't evoke some sympathy or empathy when you spend some time with them, even if that time is during a trial.

Victims react differently... I've been fortunate enough not to have ever been a victim. If I had been, I might see things about capital punishment differently.

However, the reactions of the victims vary. Some are forgiving, and some want vengeance. If requested, our judges let the victims or the families of the victims speak in court before sentence is passed. The venom spewed, the hate and the hurt, can be justified because it can be the injured party's only chance to tell the defendant what pain his or her actions have caused. There are times when there are no dry eyes in the courtroom, including the eyes of the defendant. It doesn't appear to affect the sentence, but it seems to help the victim get rid of the fury so the healing process can begin.

Lessons to be learned... I've learned a lesson from some of the families of the defendants who are in court for the sentencing, even when the crime committed was a heinous one.

I couldn't imagine that the defendant's family wasn't also horrified about what their family member had done. But then I realized they weren't condoning it, they were just there, to be there for him when he received his punishment.

Shifting penalties... The basis for acquittal or the severity of a penalty can be a reflection of the community's standards or attitude at a certain time.

Back in the early 1970s, a Kaua'i woman in the process of a divorce went to the bank and drew the money out of the joint account, took a gun, drove to a shopping center, and shot and killed her husband. She tried to kill his girlfriend, too, but the gun jammed. The judge acquitted her on the basis of a claim that she had suffered "a psychotic moment." That wouldn't happen today.

For many years, those who used and dealt drugs often got very lengthy prison terms. So many long sentences, however, led to serious overcrowding in the jails here, as it has all across the country. So while the severe penalties are still within the law, judges are allowed a certain amount of discretion and are finally meting out less harsh sentences in drug cases.

Now it's child molesters who are feeling the wrath of the court. Sexual assault cases are difficult to prove because there are rarely witnesses, so it is usually one person's word against the other's. Prosecution is especially difficult in cases dealing with children – and we do indeed have such cases here in Paradise. I think that most people, including jurors, have such a hard time imagining that someone could do such a thing to a child, that they have a hard time believing it actually happened.

Brotherly love and duty... Once there was a case involving a police officer and his kid brother. The teenager had gone on a crime spree, and then went to his big brother's house to hide after committing a whole string of burglaries. The brother/cop did his duty, turned him in, and testified against his little brother when the case went to trial.

But at sentencing, that big brother pleaded with the judge on his brother's behalf. He said he understood what the court knew about the boy, but what it didn't know was that this was also a kind, caring kid, a kid "who had gently picked up their sobbing mother and carried her home from their father's grave." By the time the officer was through explaining why he loved his brother, tears were streaming down his face.

And while this certainly wasn't the only reason, the officer resigned from the police force soon afterward. The kid brother served less than the maximum time in jail, and is now married and holds down a full-time job.

Keiki O Kaua‘i

Kaua‘i has some of the most beautiful *keiki* (children) in the world, with those great big brown eyes and jubilant spirits! The youngsters can play together for hours without any toys and few fights. They are generally left unfettered, not tied down to manners and bedtimes. Especially at parties, they run until they drop. After the backyard lu‘au, there are youngsters asleep all over the parlor floor.

Most of them grow up to be nice human beings, although if they are seeking advanced education and a good job, they usually have to leave the island in search of their fortune.

But a growing percentage of them are getting into more serious trouble. There are Hawaiian terms for three "degrees of badness" of kids. There is "humbug" or *kolohe*, which means mischievous or rascal; *pilikia*, meaning difficult, getting into some trouble; and *pilau*, a name reserved for the worst, for those who are "junk," or really bad – it's the Hawaiian word for "rotten."

Sitting on a bench outside the patrol division going over the Daily Blotter for more than 20 years, I've seen a lot of "prisoners" – in all three degrees of badness – being brought into the station.

Kolohe Kids

There were always humbug kids who skip school to go surfing and occasionally get into some scrapes, but rarely do anything to warrant more than a scolding from the police. That was especially true back when everyone knew everyone else. If those kids were ever brought to the station in a blue-and-white, they were afraid and mortified.

A love pat or an assault? A woman said she was sexually assaulted by a juvenile as she was walking down Kawaihau Rd. Investigation revealed that a boy about 11 years old and riding a bicycle, stopped, patted her on the ʻokole, said he loved her, and rode away.

A little humbug… Police responded to a report of a 4-year-old riding a motorized bike. They gave him a stern warning, and he promised he would stay off the "woad"… and a Kapaʻa woman reported that her home had been burglarized, and investigation revealed small fingerprints and candy missing.

A lesson to be learned… A 9-year-old called police (no doubt with his parents in the background), to report that he and a friend had accidentally started a fire and they couldn't put it out. The fire caused a loss to the plantation of $13,000 in cane burnt before it was ready to harvest. The boys were charged with criminal property damage (and we'd guess the judge had a serious talk with these little defendants).

Seeking the spot light… An 11-year-old boy was charged with open lewdness (flashing his ʻokole)… police got a call about elementary school boys trying to get their classmates' attention by "mooning"… and a high-school student exposed himself to a teacher.

NOT at any price... Two very young girls were counseled after it was learned that they were practicing the world's oldest profession in the plantation camps to earn money for their Girl Scout uniforms... and a man asked to speak to an officer about his teenage son (and who hasn't wanted to speak to someone about a teenager at one time or another?).

Big-time criminals... Police broke up a North Shore burglary ring when they apprehended four youngsters – ages 4, 7, 8, and 9 – who admitted to breaking into the YMCA's Camp Naue and stealing $60 worth of food. One of the youngsters was a repeat offender.

That-was-then-this-is-now... Two 5-year-olds faced felony sexual abuse charges for "tampering with a classmate," which sounds suspiciously like what used to be called "playing doctor."

A future prison cook? Two youngsters went to Kauaʻi Veterans Memorial Hospital saying they were dizzy and had OD'd. Investigation revealed that they had eaten some brownies made by another kid, who had boiled some marijuana and added it to the mix. One of the youngsters said that he had eaten two of them and that he was "stoned." Police talked to the 11-year-old baker and warned him to forget the Alice B. Toklas recipe and stick to the instructions on the box the next time he makes brownies.

The biggest chicken fight in the world: A Hanamaʻulu man called police saying that he was holding two boys, ages 7 and 8, each of whom he had caught clutching one of his prize game cocks.

But what really made the man mad was that while the kids were in his yard, they opened all the coops, and 26 chickens, each trained to fight, immediately tried to decide which cock was king of the hill. After the feathers stopped flying . . . well, they stopped flying because the birds had hurt each other so much that most of them had to be destroyed.

Police turned the boys over to the custody of their parents with appointments set for them to appear in Family Court. At that time, the judge will have a serious discussion with the boys about how their actions resulted in 26 prize game cocks being converted into $3,900 worth of chicken soup.

Kidz R Resourceful: A listing on the Daily Blotter about the theft and subsequent return of two fighting cocks led to this explanation: A police officer's talk with the father of one of the young suspects led to the sudden reappearance of the cocks, but this isn't the first such theft. It seems that some eighth-graders have been stealing the cocks and staging their own chicken fights. Sometimes they return a bird and steal another one that looks like a better fighter.

Kolohe girlz: A West side boy was probably panic-stricken at the thought of having to explain how he let some girls take his dad's car from school. The girls drove all the way to the other side of the island, up Loop Road in Wailua Homesteads, and parked next to the Wailua River, which at that point was a babbling brook.

When they couldn't get the car started again, they left to get help. While they were gone, it rained... a lot. Heavy rains caused a flash flood, the babbling brook became a raging torrent, the car went floating away and was completely destroyed in the process.

Some mis-communication... An understandably distraught mother called to say that her daughter had been driven to and from Kukui Grove in the trunk of someone's car, but investigation revealed that the whole thing was a misunderstanding. The young girl, a special education student, described riding in the back of a car where the back lifted up, but it was the back of a station wagon, so all is well.

Youngsters seek help too... a little boy went to his nearest fire station to find a friend to talk to about family problems... a Kukui'ula child called 911 to say his babysitter had left and would police please find his mother... a concerned father asked police to talk to his little girl to see if they can find out why she is so sad when she comes home from school every day... and a report came over the scanner, in hushed tones, that an infant who had appeared perfectly healthy a few hours earlier had just died.

Pilikia Kids

Even by the early 1970s, however, there was a growing number of pilikia kids. There were a lot of runaways here – kids running away from bad family situations – and kids running to drugs, sex or excitement. It was still pretty much a few kids responsible for a lot of crimes, but I started seeing more kids being brought into the station. They were embarrassed, but that didn't serve as a deterrent.

Charge it to Daddy: In an example of youthful resourcefulness, a 12-year-old but mature-looking girl treated herself and friends to meals and drinks at the Kaua'i Surf Hotel to the tune of $350. She charged all the tabs on the false claim that her father had an account at the Kaua'i Yacht Club. Police say it appears the girl had been hanging around the hotel for three weeks, eating most of her meals there, before the staff caught on that she was not a paying guest.

Why don't they just put it into T-Bills? A 16-year-old boy visiting his friend's house saw the friend's parents' personal identity number (PIN) for their business account. The boy then searched for and found their ATM card, and he was off on a spree.

He used the card to make withdrawals from different ATMs, sometimes several times a day, sometimes being photographed and sometimes not. Then he went to Honolulu and used the card there. This went on for almost a month. He had withdrawn more than $35,000 before he was caught.

Police charged him with felony theft. Although he admitted his computer-aided stealing, he had little to show for all his shopping, and so a restitution order would have done little good.

Detective Ale Quibilan, who told me about this, said while it's good the parents whose money was stolen will be reimbursed by the bank, there were several disturbing aspects to this case. One, that the security folks didn't seem too alarmed about this theft, saying the bank routinely "eats" such losses (and ultimately we'll all pay with higher banking fees); and secondly, this kid will get away with little more than a slap on the wrist, and possibly not see it as anything worse than a prank.

Kids and Easy Money

Kaua'i police received word from a California police department that two runaways – boys, 13 and 14 – might be heading for Kaua'i after a wild spending spree in San Francisco. The boys had high-rolled it in a limousine for themselves and several other junior-high school students and persuaded the limo driver to go in and register them into a $225 room at the Mark Hopkins Hotel on Nob Hill. They treated their friends to all kinds of new stereo equipment, and they paid a travel agent $5,000 in cash for a Hawaiian vacation.

Mainland police learned about the escapade when the other youngsters returned to school the next day and told everyone about their big night on the town. School officials alerted police, who in turn called the KPD. (By this time, the story had made its way into newspapers across the country.)

The KPD might have missed the boys if one of them hadn't nearly drowned in the ocean off Poʻipu. After the boy was rescued and taken to Wilcox Hospital, a police officer was called because there was no adult around. That was when it was learned that the boys arrived on Kauaʻi with about $111,000 in cash.

They also learned the boys had faked their way into a posh South Shore hotel room by telling the front desk clerk that their parents had stopped at a shopping center, given them money and told them to go ahead and get checked in.

The boys told police that they had financed their trip by taking about $120,000 in drug sale profits from a mainland apartment belonging to one of the boys' relatives. One of the boys told the KPD that he had found the money and two bags of what he thought was cocaine in a false-bottom drawer.

When the KPD called the apartment resident about the theft, he said – not surprisingly – that nothing was missing. Meanwhile, mainland police searched the apartment and found drug paraphernalia but no dope.

Police escorted the boys to their plane – they had round-trip tickets – but it's not known what kind of reception they received when their relatives met them at the mainland airport, or if they met them at the airport, or how the loser of that money will deal with his loss.

Four years later (not surprisingly), no one had stepped forward to claim the money, so under the asset forfeiture law, the KPD was able to keep most of the stolen (?) drug (?) money.

Pilau Kids

Unfortunately now, like elsewhere, there are a growing number of kids causing serious trouble. More and more often, they are younger and younger, mean-spirited defiant kids. What I see now, as the blue-and-whites pull up and the kids get out with cuffs and shackles, may be bravado, but they not only don't seem terribly upset, it's almost like it's a badge of honor. And they're capable of being sullen, sassy and combative.

I also see some families being completely destroyed by drugs, especially cocaine and methamphetamine, and most especially in families of second-generation drug users. This "village" has lost control of these children.

One day, as I was talking with some officers at KPD headquarters, we were speculating as to why some kids who get in trouble with the law apparently learn from their mistakes, outgrow it or something, while others continue getting into more and more serious trouble as they get older.

When we discussed specific cases, it appeared that the only common denominator in the latter group was that they had parents, usually a mother, who always thought it was everyone else's fault but "her Johnny's." In her many visits to the police station over the years, the mother always had an excuse. It was always a case of mistaken identity, it was his friends who did it, his friends led him astray, the witnesses are lying, the police are out to get him, and so on.

One result is more serious crime by more juveniles who

appear to feel no shame. In 1994, 17- and 18-year-old boys were charged in a near-fatal stabbing and in a (separate) gunshot murder. This would not be major news in most mainland cities, but these were unfortunate firsts for Kaua'i.

There are rumors of kids carrying guns to school but not reports of guns in the school yet. Police have been successful so far in nipping gang activities in the bud, and Police Chief George Freitas, who was a captain in gang-ridden Richmond, California, said he sees no imminent threat of gang formation and the accompanying violence.

Mea Maka'ika'i a me Mea 'auana
(VISITORS AND WAYFARERS...)

Tourism is the Garden Island's number one industry, and because the people here are basically so hospitable, Kaua'i earned the honor of being named "The Friendliest Tourist Destination in the Country" in a Condé Nast magazine survey. Most of our visitors come, relax, have fun, and leave with no problems.

But some seem to bring trouble with them (even jerks take vacations) or run into it here. Tourists often seem to do things they would never consider doing at home; they manage to get lost on a round island with only one highway; their imaginations can run wild; maybe the mai-tais are more potent than they expected; maybe it's the warmth, the colors, the vast ocean. And of course, for some local miscreants, tourists are easy targets. Whatever the case, some tourists end up on the Blotter.

No greater love... A young Japanese woman honeymooning at Club Med got into trouble while swimming not far off shore – and her new husband hurried to save her. One problem: he couldn't swim. He held her up above his head, but that left him completely submerged. He soon passed out. Fortunately, a swimming instructor saw there was a problem, swam out and brought the couple to shore, where oxygen was used to revive the gallant bridegroom.

Variation on Kama Sutra position #3206... Paramedics were called to a honeymooners' room at the Westin after the young groom, climbing over his bride in bed, slipped and rammed his knee into her face, breaking her nose.

Better to be wanted than not... A visitor went to the police station and told officers that he was wanted in Texas for auto theft and forgery and that he was tired of running. Police took him to jail and sent teletype messages to the FBI and the Houston police. But when they got no response within 48 hours, they had no choice but to let the long-suffering man go, back to being wanted.

Hugathons need permits... A tour driver carting a busload of Japanese visitors stopped at a Waimea Canyon lookout, where they encountered a group of people selling hugs for a dollar each for charity. Typically easily confused by Americans, the Japanese were even more so when confronted by smiling Kauaians with outstretched arms offering hugs for bucks. By the time the tour driver reported this weirdness to the police and the police had arrived at the scene of the... whatever it was... the hug-sellers were gone. It turned out that a few well-intentioned supporters of a local charity were making an unauthorized effort, and an illegal one without a permit, to raise money for an environmental group.

There's never a shark around when you want one... We didn't hear if the woman who called from the hotel to report that her very inebriated husband insisted on going swimming in the ocean was happy or not when he returned safely to shore.

Visitor of the Year... While examining the liquor bottles at a hotel shop, a woman from Texas dropped one and it broke. The clerk told her she would have to pay for it, and the customer made it clear that she didn't feel it was her responsibility and left in a huff. Later, when the guest was called back to the shop, she wrote a $15 check. But as she wrote it, she made insulting remarks to the clerk – and the clerk gave her one punch. It ended with an apology by the clerk (who will not receive the Aloha Spirit Award), and the customer deciding not to press charges.

Well, *here's* a vacation suggestion... Two groups of visitors who had never seen each other before got into a hassle on a boat in the lagoons at a posh hotel, and in the wake of the mutual mauling, four of them ended up with assault charges.

Reportedly, someone in a group of young people in a prenuptial party accidentally stepped on the foot of an older woman already on the boat. Apologies were made, but the older woman and her husband thought the group was too loud and they began complaining.

The noise and the complaints escalated, and the bride-to-be told police that when the older woman grabbed her by the neck, the lovely bride-to-be just shut her eyes and took a swing, cutting her hand when she knocked the woman's teeth loose. A free-for-all broke out, and three females and a male were taken to the hospital for treatment of injuries, but they were released in time for the wedding.

Kuhio Highway Ain't No Autobahn: A German visitor called police, saying he was being attacked by a Hawaiian woman who was six feet tall and weighed 300 pounds. Police found that she wasn't *quite* that large; it just seemed that way to the terrified tourist because she was one big angry *tita* who didn't like the way he was driving. She chased him to the airport, hopped out of her car, and slapped and scratched him until some security guards came to his rescue.

Any Ol' Excuse Will Do: A California visitor told police that he was returning from the North Shore when a car driven by a local person began tailgating him. He said after awhile the local driver forced him to stop and demanded $125 to buy a new muffler. The local man told the visitor that he was driving so slow, it caused his muffler to blow. An argument ensued, during which the local guy punched the visitor's wife and poured beer over her head.

(And no doubt the tourist was justifiably furious when the good ol' North Shore cop chose to believe the good ol' North Shore guy when he said, "Whoa brah, that's not what happened.")

Na Pali Trail can be - well - a *thriller*... A woman reported that when she and her husband had hiked in seven miles along Na Pali Trail, they got into an argument and her husband told her he was going to throw her off a cliff. She hiked as fast as she could on to Kalalau, where she told people that her husband had threatened to kill her. A concerned citizen swam out to a catamaran to ask for help, and the nice captain gave her a ride back to Ke'e Beach. The husband's side of the story wasn't available.

Tourist from the planet Mainland... A woman who claimed to be a "business executive from North America" told police that three men attacked her near a church in Kapaʻa town. She said they took her clothes off but were not successful in raping her. She said she was then walking nude down to Zippy's drive-in in Waipouli, and that a man came along, gave her a towel to cover herself, and drove her to her hotel.

When the desk clerk refused to give her her room key, she called police. Her initial complaint was about not getting her room key, but police learned she owed the hotel a great deal of money. Then she told police about what she said was an attempted rape, adding that she was blind at the time and couldn't see her attackers. Police did establish that a gentleman picked her up in the all-together in front of Zippy's, but that's all they could verify. When they checked the scene of the alleged attack, they found her clothing stacked neatly in a pile, along with the purse she claimed was stolen.

These things, along with other strange remarks, led police to call the state psychiatrist. He said that unless she appeared to be a threat to herself or the community, or unless she herself sought help, he couldn't help her. Police had no choice but to allow her to continue life on another planet and to list the complaint as "unfounded."

But I wanted to go to Saskatchewan... A hotel employee reported that a couple who were guests were having a terrible fight, apparently disagreeing very loudly about how to spend their vacation.

Vacation of the Year: An honest visitor from New Jersey found $800 at Lihuʻe Airport and turned it over to police. When 45 days had passed without anyone claiming it, the KPD sent the money to her. She wrote the KPD a letter of thanks for her "Christmas present."

Cows, cow patooties, cow chasers, cowboys – and magic mushrooms... Three visitors were wandering around in a large pasture in Wailua Homesteads when a herd of cattle started running towards them. The visitors chased off the cattle, which scattered in all directions.

This greatly annoyed the cowboys who had just rounded them up, and who proved to have little patience with tourist cow-chasers. The cowboys' lack of patience may result in assault charges against them – but then on the other hand, the trio of visitors may not want to explain to the judge that they were in the pasture looking for magic mushrooms, which sprout in cow paddies.

Request with punctuation... Wilcox Hospital staff treated a California man for head bruises incurred after he made too much noise during the torch-lighting ceremony at Coco Palms Hotel. When hotel manager "Big John" Kauo suggested that the man be quiet, the man instead became belligerent. Not a wise choice, given that Big John, who comes by his name legitimately, then insisted, with exclamation points embossed on the man's head, that the obnoxious tourist be quiet.

Reportedly the man chose not to press charges, but departed haughtily, saying he'd have his friend, Senator Ted Kennedy, settle this matter for him.

How will they explain the credit card bills? A couple who had just completed a seminar on Oʻahu came to Kauaʻi for a few days' vacation at a bed and breakfast in Wailua Homesteads. They asked their host to suggest hikes in secluded areas, and then they took off for the day. When they didn't return that night, the B&B host, nervous like the rest of us about hikers who fail to return, called police to report them missing. The KPD sent out an APB immediately, but the couple turned up a few hours later.

Not being aware of our cause for nervousness – two hiking visitors were murdered in that same trail some years ago – they were surprised at the amount of attention being paid their failure to return. They were also relieved to learn that the report of their "disappearance" wasn't going to be blasted across the front pages of the newspaper because they felt their respective spouses at home might not approve of their "vacation."

It was probably the wrong room... A Kapa'a hotel guest told police that someone knocked on his door. He opened it to see a big local man he'd never seen before. The man said, "You better watch out!" The visitor was so scared that he immediately packed his bags and left.

Island of Aloha... Late one night in the parking lot of a Wailua hotel, a local-appearing male approached a visiting couple and demanded their money. The couple didn't see a gun, but they feared their assailant might have one, so the man handed over what cash he had – a little more than $200 – in a money clip. The visitor asked if he could have the money clip back and the accommodating thief returned it to him, before fleeing.

I saw you the first time, OK? A woman jogging through the Kealia cane fields reported that a deviant repeatedly followed her, then raced ahead of her, stopped, and exposed himself each time as she caught up and passed him.

Far above the call of duty: A visitor – a large woman – broke her ankle while hiking Nounou Trail over Sleeping Giant mountain. It took six firemen, off-duty police Captain Brian Fujiuchi, and three other visitors – 10 people in all – to carry the hefty lady down the narrow, steep, slippery trail to paramedics waiting for her at the base of the mountain in Wailua Homesteads.

You're not supposed to eat the little umbrella: The Kaua'i Surf Hotel called police when one of its guests began screaming and climbing trees in the wee small hours of the morning. When she came down from on high, police took her to Wilcox Hospital, where she attributed her unusual behavior to a cocktail waitress who, she claimed, slipped some drugs into her drinks. Police investigated her claim but came away convinced that if she had indeed ingested any drugs, they hadn't come from the bar where she had been drinking.

Talk about having a bad day! A visitor was staying in Anahola and his wife started having difficulty breathing. He decided he could get her to Wilcox Hospital faster if he drove her there, rather than call 911, so he borrowed his friend's rental car to make the trip.

His problems really started when he almost missed the Kuhio Hwy. turn-off toward Hanama'ulu that led to the hospital. Realizing that, he then swung the wheel to the right and ran smack into the cement curbing island at that spot, and the impact activated the air bags. They survived that and he managed to pull the air bags out of their faces, but the underside of the car was wrecked from the collision. He drove on anyway and managed to make it to the top of Kapaia Hill before the car broke down all together.

The husband then jumped out and flagged down a passing car, excitedly asking the driver to take them to the hospital. The Good Samaritan accommodated them, but probably scratched his head, because all he had to do was drive around the corner to the hospital's emergency room entrance.

Fortunately, the wife's problem wasn't life-threatening and she was treated and released. Unfortunately, the man driving the car wasn't the person who signed the rental car agreement and the visitor who did sign for the car didn't take out insurance, so there's a bit of a problem determining who is going to pay for the major damages to the rental car.

A haunted rock? Mayor Eduardo Malapit received a package with a mainland return address and, having been warned about opening suspicious-looking packages, called the police and Civil Defense. As it turned out, the box contained a rock and a note from former visitors. They said they'd heard they weren't supposed to take rocks from the beach, and since they'd taken it, they'd had nothing but bad luck, and would the mayor please return it. So the mayor had Civil Defense take the rock to the dump, with the police standing by, while they disposed of it.

A different kind of room service: When the bellman at a local hotel took a couple of guests to their room, he discovered the door was chained and bolted from the inside. He went to the next room to call the front desk about the possible mix-up.

While he was talking to the desk clerk and learning that no one else was assigned to that room, a couple unchained the door and bolted down the stairs in front of the startled visitors. The bellman then went into the room, looked around and found 13 small packages of marijuana in the refrigerator. The hotel called the police, but no one could give a description of the couple, so police confiscated, photographed and destroyed the pot, which was apparently intended for sale.

It's easy to get confused... A report of a man directing traffic and causing a jam at Poʻipu Beach turned out to be a lost tourist trying to get someone to stop and give him directions to his hotel… a visitor asked for help in finding his rental car in a shopping center parking lot, lost as it was in a "sea" of look-alike rental cars… and visitors from California lost some items by putting them into the wrong rental car.

A golfer went too far... There was a report that a golf cart and driver went off a cliff at the Westin's golf course, but it turned out that just the golfer went over the cliff; a Japanese visitor had been looking for his golf ball, fell about 25 feet, but was lucky to be without his cart and suffered only cuts and bruises… a visitor from Oregon lost his wallet, and some honest soul turned it into police; but a few minutes after retrieving it from the police station, the embarrassed visitor called back to say he had lost it again… and police helped a visitor sleeping in the bellman's cart at the Islander Inn back to her room.

Well-intentioned embarrassment... A visitor at the Westin's Palace Court restaurant reported a fire, which was actually the shadow of flames dancing on the wall, cast by a Sterno container beneath a chafing dish… and visitors at the Coconut Marketplace reported people stuffing what appeared to be a body into a truck, but police investigation revealed it was a golf bag.

Glossary

"Yes, Chief?"

Whenever you see an ʻokina (a backwards apostrophe), it signifies a glottal stop, and a pronounciation similar to the sound between the ohs in the English oh - oh. It's used only before vowels, although not in all words. Unfortunately the ʻokina is too often omitted in spelling and pronouncing Hawaiian words. This is a mistake because it sometimes changes the meaning of words otherwise spelled the same. For example: *Ono* is a type of fish, while *'ono* means delicious; *au* is a period of time, while *'au* is to swim.

Mixed in are a few pidgin words or local phrases.

affray: fight – but not used much anywhere else but Hawai'i.

'aina: (Ay-Nah) the land

akamai: (ah-kah-MY) smart, clever

auwe: (ow-WAY) oh! oh dear! alas! used as a moan or groan, or to grieve

brah, blah: brother

chicken skin: pidgin English for goose bumps or gooseflesh

da kine: like "you know"… that time, that thing, that guy

estray: on the mainland it's usually used as "stray"

estray bovine: cow out for a stroll

grines: grinds, local food - 'ono grines: delicious local food

hale: (Hah-le) house

haole: (how-leh) white person, originally anyone to whom local customs were foreign

humbug: also kolohe or rascal, makes trouble

kama'aina: (kah-mah-EYE-nah) those born in Hawai'i or those who have lived here a long time

kane: (KAH-neh) male or husband

kokua: (KOH-koo-ah) to provide help or assistance

imu: (ee-moo) hole dug in the ground and used as a steam oven

kalua: (KAH-loo-ah) the way pigs or turkeys are prepared in the imu

kapakahi: (kah-pah-KAH-hee) crooked, cockeyed, uneven

Kaua'i: (cow-ah ee): the Garden Island; to dry in the sun; forthcoming with food

kuleana: (koo-leh-Ah-na) a special interest, right, privilege or responsibility

lanai: (LAH-nye) porch or covered pavilion

laulau: steamed pork and butterfish wrapped in taro shoot and ti leaves

lei: (LAY) garland of flowers or seeds

lu'au: (LOO-ow) Hawaiian feast, originally called aha'aina

lychee: (LIE-chee) tree-grown fruit originally from China

mahalo: (mah-HAH-loh) thank you

mahalo nui loa: thank you very much

makai: (mah-KYE) toward the sea

malihini: (mah-le-hee-nee) stranger, newcomer, guest

manini: (mah-nee-nee) slang for stingy, small, petty

mauka: (MAU-kah) toward the mountains

'ohana: (oh-hah-nah) family, kin group, related or extended family

'okole: (OH-ko-ley) buttocks

'ono: (OH-noh) tastes delicious

ono: (oh-noh) popular white meat fish (aka wahoo), listed on every menu

opu: (oh-POO) abdomen

pakalolo: (pah-kah-LO-lo) marijuana (from weed and crazy)

paniolo: (pah-nee-OH-lo) cowboy; from the Hawaiian word for Espanol, and referring to the Spanish-speaking cowboys who came to Hawai'i to work the cows on the ranches here

pau: (pow) all done, over with

pau hana: (pow hah-nah) finished or quit (pau) work (hana)

pilikia: (pee-lee-KEE-ah) cause trouble (more than humbug but less than pilau)

poi: (POY) paste made from kalo or taro root; staple in Hawaiian diet

puka: (POO-ka) hole

pupu: (POO-POO) "little things," snacks, i.e., won ton, raw fish (sashimi or poke), delicacies from different ethnic groups, usually served with drinks

saimin: (sigh-min) Japanese noodle soup

taro: (TAH-ro) staple vegetable of Hawai'i whose root is baked and pounded into poi; actual Hawaiian word is kalo. Taro is an ancient pronunciation brought from Tahiti.

tita: (TEE-tah) pidgin English for sister; usually refers to a formidable, tough-sounding female, i.e., "she's one tita" or "titah;" but said softly can also be a term of endearment

wahine*:* (wah-HEE-neh) female or wife

wai: (y) fresh water (as opposed to kai which means salt water, ocean)

And my own personal favorite:

true fack: the opposite of "wrong misinformation"

Aloha: love, kindness, hello and goodbye.

MAIL ORDER

Police Blotter, *Kauaʻi Style,* by Georgia Mossman

Number of Books _____ @ 14.95 (+$6 shipping)

Make check or money order to:

Ka Hui Kanelimu Publishing
5968 Heamoi Place
Kapaʻa, HI 96746

Books should be mailed to:

Name: _____

Address: _____

_____

_____

Mahalo nui loa!

Georgia Mossman

What others are saying about this book:

"This is really not a story of crime on the Garden Island. Instead, it speaks of a quieter time; of living in a small town with its requisite number of town characters and misfits. It's a story told with sly humor mixed with touches of poignancy and sadness.

"A great book and one that gives you more of a feeling for Kaua'i, this wonderful little island out in the middle of the Pacific, than most tourist guide books."

Chief George Freitas
Kaua'i Police Department

"Police Blotter, Kaua'i Style,' is a delightful historic journey through our annals of crime. The outrageous antics reported left me laughing and crying at the same time. The cartoons are a hoot! Georgia Mossman's book is like a welcomed rain in the literary drought the island has suffered since her retirement from **The Garden Island newspaper.***"*

Jim Jung,
Kauai's Public Defender

"Georgia is a warm and caring person with a good eye for details. She has an excellent memory and many times offered or suggested 'ideas' that linked one crime to another, that led to an arrest.

"Good detectives are a special 'breed' that can sense when something is not right or when someone is not quite telling the truth. Georgia displayed these same qualities in doggedly tracking down a story, whether it involved a petty theft or a class A felony.

"In my book, Georgia is an 'honorary detective extraordinaire.'"

Chief Brian Fujiuchi (ret.)
Kaua'i Police Department